~~SUICIDE~~

Helping you and your friends to live

SPECIAL TEEN EDITION of "Why They Die"

written by
Jerry Johnston,
D.Min.

with Don
Simmonds

FOR VIDEOS AND RESOURCES, VISIT CROSSROADS360.COM

NOT SUICIDE: Helping You and Your Friends
To Live

Jerry Johnston, D. Min. with Don Simmonds

Published by Crossroads Christian Communications
Inc.
1295 North Service Road P.O. Box 5100
Burlington, ON L7R 4M2
crossroads.ca

Cover & Interior Design: Laura MacDermid
Editors: Danny Zacharias, Diane Roblin-Lee
ISBN: 1-896930-52-7

Printed in Canada

CONTENTS

CROSSROADS CHRISTIAN COMMUNICATIONS INC.

Crossroads Chairman and CEO Don Simmonds celebrated the 50-year fruitful ministry of founders, David and Norma Jean Mainse, at a recent historic Gala with ministry friends and supporters. *100 Huntley Street*, the flagship television program of Crossroads, began on June 15, 1977, and is the longest running daily Christian television program in Canada. Crossroads provides relevant messages of faith and inspiration for millions of Canadians and people around the world. Crossroads interacts with its viewers via 24/7 Prayer Lines, and it has also been a highly respected and effective not-for-profit aid agency for over 25 years, having responded in times of natural disaster worldwide, raising funds and partnering with on-site, non-government organizations for emergency relief and long-term rebuilding strategies.

Don Simmonds leads the exciting vision for the future through a dramatic expansion of Crossroads ministries by reaching all ages at all stages with the effective increase of media programs and content harnessing all media platforms. *Crossroads 360* is a multiple-channel online media service, connecting to nearly four billion people globally by creatively proclaiming faith and values. As an extension of our mission, we have launched *Crossroads USA* to touch all of North America for Jesus Christ.

Crossroads Centre Prayer Lines, **1-866-273-4444** (available in Canada and the United States), are available 24/7 to minister to you and help you follow Jesus Christ. Visit our ministry website at **crossroads.ca.** Peruse our e**store** to obtain excellent resources to build your faith. Go to **crossroads360.com** for all of our online video resources and search by topic, need, or question. Be sure to send us your questions or prayer requests through **crossroads360.com**

When you are in the Burlington area, stop by for a visit at the Crossroads Centre for individual prayer or a tour of our studios: **Crossroads, PO Box 5100, Burlington, Ontario L7R 4M2**

We count it an honor to serve and strengthen you in your walk with God.

crossroads

ACKNOWLEDGEMENTS

Mark Twain once wrote, *"Ideally a book would have no order to it, and the reader would have to discover his own."* The origin and order of this book deserves a great deal of gratitude.

Don and Fay Simmonds—thank you for your tireless efforts for young people for so many years. You both epitomize how much a couple can do who truly care.   Don, thank you for your challenging vision for Crossroads coupled with such a passionate, caring heart.

Gary Gerard, thank you for your wisdom on behalf of the supporters and friends of Crossroads, and being so sensitive to find just the right resources to build their faith and evangelistic fervor. You are a faithful and good brother.

Cristie Jo and Jenilee, thank you for the many hours of reviewing the manuscript and making so many helpful suggestions. Cristie Jo, you are my best friend and soul mate!

Laura MacDermid, exceptionally talented Creative Lead at Crossroads, thank you for going the extra mile and shaping this book to be a resource, help, and guide to youth and parents everywhere.

Rick and Karla Moore, two of my dearest friends, who have stood so close to Cristie and me. Endless thanks. Karla combed through the manuscript and provided helpful ideas and corrections.

Danny Zacharias, lecturer in Biblical studies and technology assistant, at my alma mater, Acadia University Divinity College, for proofing the manuscript.

David Mainse, a man whose life is distinguished by such abundant spiritual fruit. Thank you for caring for lost, meandering people and having the vision to establish a Prayer Centre Hotline, 1-866-273-4444 so many years ago. Thank you for your compassion, and your tears for men and women who need Christ.

DEDICATION

This book is dedicated to my young friend
Dylan French, age 20, who represents the
incredible potential God created in
young people everywhere.

It is my prayer that not one other young
person will ever decide life is not worth living.

~ *Don Simmonds*

CHAPTER 1

COACH DON AND DYLAN

"Friends, it's time to put our anchors down.
Goodbye, Dyl."

Imagine having worked hard to get good enough marks to become a doctor. You stayed disciplined in university to get into Med school. You gave up everything to pass your medical exams and finally, became an MD! You've had the opportunity to work with some very experienced doctors who have taught you everything they know. You have gained deep experience now and are able to save many lives.

One day, just as your shift at the hospital began, you were bound and gagged and unable to assist as patient after patient came into the emergency room. You could not help them. Instead you were forced to watch as they struggled in their pain, and without assistance, ultimately died. You just knew you could have helped save them, but forces outside of your control held you back from doing the very thing your life was meant to do.

My wife Fay and I live in a small community and met in high school when we were just 16 years old. From the time we were married 4 years later, the well-being of young people has been a priority in our lives. We have four children. We have led our church youth group. I've coached hockey for 20 years. We just love helping teenagers transition to adulthood with purpose and with character so they can lead the best possible life. One could say, it is why we exist.

Currently I consider it a privilege to be the head coach of the Uxbridge Tigers, our community's high school varsity hockey team. Our motto is to "win at hockey and win in life" so we work hard to model and teach character and broaden what it means to be a whole hockey player; admiring more than the hockey skills of our players, but also their intellectual development, physical well-being, relationships, and inner self.

You can imagine how devastating it was when we received word that Dylan, a former hockey player, took his own life early one January morning. With a goal to help my players "win in life" and now this? Dylan had his whole life ahead of him. He was loved by his parents and sister. Dylan had many friends. He was talented athletically and musically. And I was his coach, feeling like the doctor who had the ability to help, but held out of reach for some reason. And this inability to help him in his time of need lives on with me now.

Suicide, among teens, has become epidemic. I don't ever want to lose another young friend, like Dylan, to suicide. So I would like to use whatever means available, to make sure you and your friends know that you are precious to God and that your life, no matter what challenges you face, is worth living!

That is the reason for this book.

Let me tell you more about my friend, Dylan. He was a true Tiger. Here is the story of our team's trip to Lake Placid, to play in the American Cup, a well known High School Tournament.

We are from Uxbridge, Ontario, a very small town of 10,000 with just one high school. We were returning to the Lake Placid Tournament for the second time since the school had established a hockey team. In the first excursion several years earlier, both our boys' and our girls' teams had taken the gold. ("No pressure" as we say in the world of sports!)

We were clearly outmatched, and had to

admit to ourselves that we were the undisputed underdogs. It would take a miracle to stay in for the playoff rounds, let alone win the whole tournament!

We were well along our 8 hour journey. Up to this point, it had been a fairly usual bus trip for a high school hockey team—full of fun and frolic, a few bad jokes and eager competitions for room team points.

We were about to watch the movie, *Miracle*, about the United States men's hockey team, led by head coach Herb Brooks (Kurt Russell), who won the gold medal in the 1980 Winter Olympics in Lake Placid, New York. Everyone on our bus had watched the movie many times. In fact, some of the guys could even give coach Herb Brooks' famous speech *verbatim*.

It was the story of an underdog USA team ending up in the gold medal game against the heavily favoured Soviet team, who had won nearly every world championship and Olympic tournament since 1954. The USA team's victory over the Soviets, in the gold medal round, had been dubbed the *"Miracle on Ice"* and in 1999, was named, by Sports Illustrated, the "Top Sports Moment of the 20th Century!"

Now we were headed to Lake Placid, where

our games would be played in that same Olympic complex; some of the contests on the very same ice surface, now called *The Herb Brooks Arena*, in which that "miracle" had taken place. As the underdogs, we needed a miracle ourselves!

My young friend, Dylan, was our goalie. It was his last year of high school, just a month or so from his last game as a Tiger. He had been a key player of our Varsity team for three years. For Dylan and this group of young men, I suspect what was about to happen, would be one of their best hockey memories ever.

We were playing teams stronger than we were, but every game was close. We won two and tied one of our first three division games, scoring only two goals in each game. If you've experienced a points tournament, you know the drill. That tied division game meant we had to battle for the right to go on to the finals.

It was Saturday night, our fourth and final division game, and the tournament was painfully close. We had to win or we'd go home. To make matters worse, we knew we would have to win by a margin of three goals. Ending up with a win by even two goals would send us home.

Now, you have to understand, for those of us who were involved in coaching and organizing the team, *winning* at hockey is not the main focus of our efforts with the young men of the Uxbridge Tigers (and believe me, we hate losing). Our coaching staff were all community volunteers, most of us being former students of Uxbridge High School. At this point, we've been together for 10 years; a dairy farmer, an emergency nurse, our former Principal, a committed teacher/coach and my son, Craig. Craig lobbied the school to start the team in his final year; as a result he is a first-year team alumnus. We do our best to use sports to help young men learn important character traits such as respect, responsibility, courage, honesty, gratitude and optimism. Each of the players carry the responsibility for one of 14 character traits throughout our season, helping the whole team live out their assigned traits in practical ways. Our "goal" is to help each of them become a *"whole"* hockey player, where the specific training and skills of hockey are just one of five parts. The four other areas of focus are: their physical well-being (including sleep and nourishment), intellectual and academic development, relationships (with teammates, friends, family and authorities) and a positive sense of self (self identity, self worth, self confidence and their spiritual self).

This background is important to this story because of what happened in Saturday night's game. We had just three minutes left in a seesaw battle that was tied 0-0. There I was, pacing up and down the bench, with obvious concern written all over my face...when I heard Kyle Arbour, #13, say, "Hey Coach, remember the trait of *optimism!*"

Having played 42 minutes with no goals scored, and knowing we *had* to score three while holding them to zero, I chuckled as Kyle applied his appointed character trait—the very way I'd asked him to!

Sure enough, with just two minutes to go, big Pete Luinstra, #7, sniped a rising shot that picked the upper right hand corner of the net. It was 1-0. But a mere win would not do the job. There were 50 seconds left, and the face-off was in our opponent's end. Our best strategy coach, Mr. Evans, set up the plan with our Captain, Tavis Smith, #11 (who usually played defense), taking the face off, with big Pete coming through the circle. The play worked perfectly, and Pete picked up the languishing puck and sniped that rising shot in the other top corner. 2-0!

With the other team coming back hard, the puck drifted into our end. Even before it happened, everyone knew what was on goalie Dylan's mind; we could tell he was going to skate out and play the puck—one of his specialties. I wish I could say he passed it up and we scored the final goal … but I can't. Dyl actually mishandled the puck right at that crucial moment; the other team's player picked it up and shot at our open net!

In a classic Dylan moment, we all watched as he dove back with a full stick extension and stopped that (otherwise) certain goal. But he didn't stop there; he played the puck again, this time successfully up to our center and top goal scorer, Mike Ramsey, #27, who, with just 24 seconds left, made one of his famous moves on their goalie and roofed the backhand game winner—putting us into the final playoff round on Sunday morning!

All the marks of a Tiger converged in that three minutes of hockey—three minutes and a tournament win none of us will ever forget. Our boys went out and dominated the highest rated team in the final game with a 2-0 conclusive win. Uxbridge Tigers hockey lore says the win that day made their coach cry *real* tears. (But, of course, what happens in a hockey dressing room stays in a hockey dressing room!)

For each of the players, this tournament, and the gold medal win, marked one of their very best hockey memories.

****

Early in the morning, on January 6th, just over two years after our Lake Placid experience, I received a text message, and then confirmed the terrible news. Dyl had taken his own life. He had returned home late the night before and, in the early hours of the morning, took a rope and hung himself in a small subdivision forest a few houses away from his. Word spread within our small community and soon the phone was buzzing with calls from other coaches. Emotions were high and there was little to say; we were stunned and speechless with the reality of the news.

Dylan had played hockey with his friends during the week. He had been at a Toronto Maple Leaf game just the night before, with his girlfriend. He was due to return to his second semester classes at university the next day. All had seemed normal.

Dylan's mom and dad asked if I would do the eulogy at the funeral. It was one of the most difficult things I have ever done. I am going to share with you what I said, as I faced my surviving hockey team, dressed in their Tigers jerseys— and hundreds in our community, searching for answers, wondering why:

Good afternoon, friends. On behalf of everyone gathered here, and those unable to be present in person today, may I say first to Jamie, Cheryl and Nicole, and their extended family, how very sorry we are for this indescribable loss. I am unable to come up with words that can adequately convey the deep sense of grief your community feels with you.

Dylan embraced life; his family and friends were his world.

Most people who crossed paths with Dyl quickly drew similar conclusions. Dylan was incredibly unique, incredibly talented, incredibly intense and incredibly fun. His interests and abilities spanned many worlds within, and outside, our small community. Last Friday, news spread quickly, traversing wide networks of family, friends, musicians, teachers, churches, teammates, employers and so many whom his life has touched. Just look at the outpouring of love and support here today. You can see what I mean.

It is a privilege for me to honour Dylan this afternoon.

I would like to talk very directly to you today. I have to say that Dylan's passing, at age 20, just starting the prime of life—and the way Dylan died—is the ultimate tragedy for any family, any group of friends, and indeed, for any community. In honouring Dylan today, the French family has asked that we consider, honestly, the implications of Dylan's life—and death—with a view to avoiding such tragedy in the future. It is only in avoiding more tragedy, that Dylan's death might accomplish some purpose.

The name Dylan, is Welsh for "man of the sea." He was well-named, because Dyl loved anything to do with water. He loved times at the cottage, swimming, sailing and waterskiing. He also loved visiting his cousins in Lunenberg, Nova Scotia. He used to dive down for scallops in the 53-degree Atlantic and would outlast everyone else in the frigid water.

And there was the musical Dylan. He loved music and its freedom of expression. Early on, he had a vision, with his band, to impact society with messages conveyed through music. Many of you will know the band, "In Lights," as they recorded and played their music, once heading to eastern Canada on tour. Guys, he loved doing music with you.

Then there was the suave Dylan; it seemed even before the bus would stop at an arena, he would have the text address of the best-looking timekeepers at the tournament. ...And his female friends were important in his life at a relatively young age; he was such a cool guy to be with. And Katie, our sympathies are extended to you.

There was the friend Dylan; he had an ability to traverse many friend-groups, past and present, often as the life of the party. His friends knew Dylan's complex—and sometimes conflicting— qualities: intense but lighthearted, thoughtful but fun, at times so focused, yet at times so easily distracted. One of the attractive things about Dylan was his interest in the deeper aspects of life—why something was unfair, or what might be done about an issue. This often made friendships with him heavy, yet meaningful. This was, indeed, an intriguing aspect of Dylan the friend.

And then there was Dylan, "defender of justice." He was always standing up for the little guy, or someone who was getting shafted. If you Google Dylan's name, you will find the first entry is his interview with the newspaper, defending a teacher at the school. If he felt someone was being attacked, he would be right there, defending the person. I remember him coming to our rescue, as coaches at a tournament, when our team was fighting within itself in the dressing room. We were trying to explain that a lack of unity would result in certain defeat... and, in grade 10, he stood up

to his older peers to defend the concept of unity...
even when as coaches, we were in the minority at
that moment.

Which brings me to Dylan, straight up. A
tough, but refreshing, part of relating to Dylan was
his direct and straightforward way. He 'was who
he was' and most people around him respected
him for that, while at the same time, running into
it head on, at some point in their relationship
with him. In fact, he would expect me to be direct
and candid in speaking with you today, without
sugarcoating this very situation.

There was Dylan, the competitor and
teammate. Everyone would agree he was the best
of teammates, one who would leave everything on
the ice for his team. He was intensely competitive;
he hated to lose, was naturally talented and was
able to walk in and perform with little preparation.
Goalies often have unique personalities, and Dylan
sure did. One didn't know really what to say during
the preparation time for a game. Sometimes, he
would want to fool around, and other times, often
abruptly, he would want solitude to gain focus.
He'd warm up his catching hand with tennis
balls off the walls in his own, custom-made drill.
Regardless, his teammates played confidently,
and played well, when he had their backs as their

goalie.

And there was Dylan, a brother. He was proud of you, Nicole. He loved seeing how hard you worked at school and hockey. He was proud of your achievements. Interestingly, he was very proud of how clearly you saw things about his life, even though you did not often agree with him. In fact, while he struggled in his own choices, he was incredibly impressed at how solid your own personal standards and faith decisions had become.

And Dylan, the son. God created the teenage years as the passage between childhood to adulthood. For Mr. and Mrs. French and Dylan, this has not been a smooth road. Having drawn a line on what was allowed, or not allowed, in their home (which, by the way, is not only their right, but their responsibility) Dylan decided to move out in grade 10. It was an anxious time, but I noticed Cheryl always brought his equipment for him to the arena. And Jamie and Cheryl, while there's lots you would do differently (like all of us parents), Dylan loved you, even through these disagreements. It's just that he didn't always show it. He knew, down deep, it was your love for him, that was at the root of these challenges. I know he knew of your love, because he told me so.

Dylan was selected as a goalie for the Uxbridge Tigers Varsity team in grade 10. Not many grade 10's are selected, because the Varsity team goes right up to second year grade 12's. This tells you something about Dyl. In grade 11, we were forced to cut Dylan, as he rolled in to the tryouts, out of shape and unprepared, assuming his strong participation in grade 10, automatically earned him a spot in grade 11.

But in grade 12, Dylan was back again, intent on making the team that did not take him the year before. And he came eager, tenacious, sharp, alert, in shape and was an obvious selection for the next two years. And this tells you a lot about Dyl.

Dylan carried all five marks of a Tiger.

- *He was alert.*

- *He played with heart.*

- *He used his head.*

- *He was a great team player.*

- *And, he loved winning so much, that he hated losing.*

I first met Dylan during an interview process that we conduct with each player trying out for the team. We have a series of questions we ask, and one is, "what is your biggest life challenge right now?" Often, the answers range from poor grades, to trying to come up with enough money for hockey. But in Dylan's case, he shared, very honestly, that he was on a search for life's meaning. He had put his life in God's hands a year earlier, but was finding it difficult to make his day-to-day choices God's way. We appreciated his openness and honesty. I explained that I had lived through the same experience as a young man in grade 10. And this created a certain bond between us.

As I speak to you today, it is almost impossible for me to believe Dylan is not with us. That such a unique and special young man, with so much potential, so much to live for—so much to offer to our world—won't be able to fulfill his purpose. It's just beyond belief.

Jamie, Cheryl, Nicole—a Tiger is never forgotten. And today we are retiring Dylan's jersey, #29, out of respect for our missing player.

I must admit to being troubled with my own lack of assistance to Dylan in his time of need. You see, our Tiger's hockey motto is to help our players "win at hockey and win in life." I can't help feeling like a coach who has deeply failed my player... where we won at hockey, but not in life—and of the two, winning in life is far more important!

The way Dylan's life ended disturbs us all. I am not one who feels Dylan was right to choose this path. Instead, I believe that life itself, is the greatest gift each of us is given. You and I have the most sacred responsibility to value our lives, with a view to becoming everything we were intended to be. There is never a reason, good enough, to yield to life's pressures and end our lives on purpose... no matter how great those pressures become. I urge you today, never to allow yourself, ever, to think this could possibly be the right choice for you. Slam the door shut on that option for the rest of your life. In fact, I wish I had added one more character trait, called "live," and I wish I had assigned that one to Dylan.

In the last five years, we have lost 13 precious young lives from our school, 3 to suicide. These are the sons and daughters of our Uxbridge community. Trying to make sense of this, especially for those in Dylan's age group, has been very difficult. So many tragic events can impact a person, and cause them to lose hope. We cannot let this happen. You must not let this happen.

Could we take this outcome of Dylan's decision and turn it into some good? We can help find real purpose to his life by committing, right here and now, never, ever, to give up on life!

This is why I dream of a community whose young men and women know the difference between right and wrong.

This is why I dream of a community whose young men and women encourage each other to make the wisest choices.

This is why I dream of a community whose young men and women voluntarily respond to that challenge from each other.

This is why I dream of a community whose young men and women see the importance of following the guidance of their parents, teachers and those trying to help them.

Dylan's decision raises so many questions. Difficult questions. Unanswerable questions. But, those closest to Dylan feel he was caught in an epic battle we all face, a battle of two worlds that are after our souls.

Just like we have a physical body that you can touch and feel, and a mind, complete with a unique personality and set of emotions, we also have a spiritual dimension. ...Some deny its existence, of course, but it is as real as our physical and emotional dimensions.

God, Himself, created you for a specific purpose. You are not an accident. Your unique differences and abilities are designed for something only you can do. It is finding that purpose that give us hope and optimism, even in the face of life's troubles, or the unfair circumstances that are sure to come to us all.

So, you need to know that destructive forces will work life-long to distract and disrupt your quest for this ultimate life purpose for which you were created. God's original design and plan for you is one that is hopeful, purposeful and for your good. But many people, not just young people, are looking for hope and purpose in the wrong places. Our dear friend, Dylan, got caught between these two worlds... and ultimately lost his hope for living.

No one has to get caught in between.

Dylan's love for boating made me think of an example to help us make sure Dylan's death does not contribute to this despair, but instead, brings a whole new sense of hope within our community. A boater has no difficulty understanding the importance of an anchor when the weather gets rough. If one does not use a solid anchor, his or her boat could drift into a perilous situation and get lost at sea. It's the same in our lives. But not one of us have to get lost in the sea of life, because God has promised to anchor us, so that not one of us will ever have to face what Dylan did.

As a final tribute to our missing friend, and to make sure the tragedy of Dylan's death actually brings new hope, I want you always to remember a verse from the Bible, found in Hebrews 6:19:

"This hope [in God] is a strong and trustworthy anchor for our souls."

I need that hope in my life. Dylan needed that hope. You need, and can have, this hope as well. It will hold you solid and secure, through the storms of life.

Friends, its time to put our anchors down.

Good bye, Dyl.

CHAPTER 2
||||||||||||||||||||||||||||||||||||||||||||||||||

"DAD, I'M GOING TO KILL MYSELF."

"Jerry, we'll do something. Son, please hold on. What can I do?"

People often ask me why I am so passionate about helping both youth and adults who exhibit suicidal tendencies. My own story will help you understand the profound compassion I have for people who are filled with utter despair, many of whom are seriously contemplating suicide. Everyone has a story to tell. By honestly sharing life's most challenging experiences, and how they are overcome, we connect immediately with —and help—those who struggle. I have never concealed how utterly confused and lost I was as a teenager, nor how truly dire was my outlook on life. I believe transparency and vulnerability are the connection points, in allowing me to bond with millions of kids worldwide, who sit riveted, identifying with similar issues.

At fourteen, alone and miserable, I laid at

one end of the sofa in our family room, feeling like the dark paneled walls were caving in on me. My parents and four brothers were away at work and school; all of them totally unaware of the tormenting battle raging within me. In my limp and lethargic state, I laid there for the longest time, almost catatonic, with my eyes intensely focused on the telephone in the distance near the kitchen. I believed it to be the final means of contact for help before ending my life. I felt nauseated and confused, convinced there was no way out of the misery I suffered. Weary from enduring months of physical and emotional torment from all the partying, drug use, and rebellion toward adult authorities in my life, I sensed an eerie and uncontrollable force, compelling me to take that final destructive turn down a dead end street, and end it all. At that point, the only thing that seemed to make any sense, was death. My emotions were unstable. My mind took me to a place where I could see myself lying in a coffin, peaceful, and finally at rest. This seemed to be a logical consequence and fitting conclusion to my failed attempt at life.

I lay there on the sofa, tightly wrapped in my dad's big light blue bathrobe. From the time I had come home from one of my first hospital stays, I had worn that ugly, oversized robe. It wasn't so much from being physically cold, as a silent cry for help, or perhaps my feeble attempt to feel closer to my father, with whom I could not communicate. Before my two hospitalizations, suspicion, mistrust, and arguments had marred our relationship and created an icy condition between us. Whenever Dad disciplined me, and that was often, I would threaten to turn him in to the authorities for child abuse. But the onset of my physical problems soon changed that warlike environment. Eventually, instead of screaming at me, my parents would console me, insisting, "Everything is all right, everything is going to get better." Sadly, things did not get better; I became more withdrawn, even docile.

With Mom and Dad both at work, and my four brothers at school, my thoughts were running wild. The antique clock on the mantel ticked to the beat of my bizarre, almost overwhelming thoughts of killing myself.

Slowly, my eyes shifted from focusing on the telephone, toward the television, where my mother had neatly displayed individual family pictures in decorative frames. Something compelled me to raise my listless body from the sofa and sluggishly pace over to the television. One by one, I picked up each picture and studied the faces of family members who seemed so out of my reach. Johnny, my oldest brother with such a gentle nature, was five years my senior. I felt I barely knew him. Next was Jay's picture; it instantly took me back to the time when we would sleep outside my parents' bedroom door at night whenever they would fight.

Then I came to the picture of Jeff, the brother to whom I was closest, not only in age, but relationally. Gazing at Jeff's image, I recalled how (despite his early attempts to protect me) his destructive lifestyle first introduced me to the drug scene. I would often find him down in our basement, dividing pounds of dope into nickel bags, dimes, and lids. I remembered the scales used for measuring hash. Jeff told me about *Kief*, a pure form of marijuana. Just two or three hits and the highs were super sensational. Jeff's enticing description was tempting, and I had responded with a giddy excitement, anticipating the time I would say yes to this alluring drug. To my surprise, Jeff reacted with an immediate threat. He said, "If you ever touch this stuff, I'll kill you. Do you understand?" I reflected on Jeff's sales ability in pushing drugs at our high school. I both loved him and hated him at the same time.

Peering at the picture of Joel, my youngest

sibling, I felt really bad. He was such a good kid to have two brothers who were doing drugs. I wondered how it might impact his future. Finally, I found myself almost hypnotized by the picture of my mom and dad. I asked myself what it would do to them if I carried out my plans. It forced me to think back to the way all my misery began.

The Johnston family fit perfectly into the upper-middle-class stereotype. We lived in Johnson County, Kansas, which, at the time, was one of the most affluent counties in the nation. My father was quite successful as a national sales director of a company with offices around the country. My artistic mother was an interior decorator. Our home was a beautiful residence situated next to a golf course. We were country club people.

My life was filled with all the typical, self-centered behavior of most unruly teenagers. I would get together with my best friend, Bill, and we would do crazy things, like interrupt the golf games of the men who regularly played the course, infuriating them. We would gorge ourselves at the clubhouse restaurant and charge it to my parent's account. The only thing I cared about was having fun and moving as fast as possible.

My dad's attempt at forming any kind of real

relationships with his five sons was lacking. His way of communicating with me and my brothers was bringing home surprise gifts; things like an air hockey game, a jukebox, and an electronic bowling machine. Since I was obsessed with *things*, I took advantage of his spoiling us. One time when he returned from a rather lengthy trip, I woke in the morning to discover a brand new motorized mini-bike perfectly positioned on the white carpet of our living room.

I could not talk to my parents about the real issues. They were typical parents—out of touch, antiquated in their thinking—the very epitome of "straight." My dad, with his pseudo-religiosity, sometimes disgusted me. Mom and Dad were so gullible; they had no idea what I was getting into.

Church was seldom part of our lives. When we did attend, it was incredibly boring. The minister preached a lifeless, denominationally-correct sermon that lulled the frigid congregants to sleep. I called it the First Church of the Deep Freeze. Although I wasn't far off, going to church was the socially acceptable Johnson County thing to do, so we did it. I remember watching my dad taking notes during the sermon. What in the world did he find interesting enough to write down in those little spiral notebooks that filled boxes he stored in his closet?

Occasionally, Dad would convince me to attend the evening youth meeting at church. He would drop me off, but as soon as the taillights of his car left the parking lot, I would leave. One time, a friend and I stole some money from an elderly woman's purse at church, picked up a couple of girls, and left for some real fun.

When the school year began, I sized up the situation almost immediately. There were two dominant self-proclaimed student groups. The "jocks" were the more athletically inclined. They were the drinkers. And then, there were the "freaks," the kids who did drugs and were proud of it. I got involved with the latter group. Every day, before and after classes, we would hang out at a place across the street from the school which we creatively called, "Across the Street." This was the place you would go, before and after the dances at school, to do drugs or get drunk. The freaks were a wild bunch of kids, but they made me feel like I belonged, and I liked that. Many of the kids would hit on joints until seconds before the final bell rang. None of the faculty ever came over. Some were probably too afraid, but most seemed downright apathetic. More than once, I heard snide remarks about "poor little rich kids" and "dumb dopers." And it was all true.

Now I can see, that a dangerous rebellion toward authority, particularly toward my parents, began in those days. Maybe it was subliminal from the crowd I hung with. My "friends" were stoners; they were eager to convert me to their way of living and having fun.

Profanity and offensive speech became my new language. My friends became more important than my "old man" or "old lady." It's hard to imagine now, that I could have referred to my parents that way. I grew in defiant boldness; telling my parents to shut up, get out of my room or leave me alone. As the weeks passed, each new day ended with me adding another brick to the wall I was building between us. I condemned them for being so "out of touch" and didn't want anything to do with them. In retrospect, it was totally unfair. I had two of the finest parents a kid could ever want; I just didn't know it at the time.

Living in a world of druggie friends, led to serious issues at school. I had absolutely no ambition with regard to education, so my grades suffered. I mouthed off to one teacher and was permanently ejected from her class. At the all-school, anti-drug assemblies, I would sit up in the bleachers and ridicule the speakers. While one expert warned about the horrors of drug addiction, I joked to my friends, "If only we could get that guy high, he would see how much fun he's missing." I spiraled out of control until I finally got kicked out of five of my seven classes. I was even ejected from study hall—how do you do that?

For five hours every day, I occupied a special chair in the school office, because of my delinquent behavior. I was told my days at that particular school were numbered. Near the end of the school year, the principal called my parents in, and informed them that I would not be allowed to return in the fall. As one would expect, the ride home that day was volcanic. My dad was irate and lectured me the entire time— but his words did not faze me one bit.

The only redeeming thing was that summer was here, and that meant I would spend my days and nights hanging around with my friends, as usual, doing nothing constructive. Mostly, we lounged around at the pool and club, smoking, swearing and condemning anything, or anyone, that did not match up to our strange standards of coolness. However, in scarce and quiet moments, I spent time wondering what would happen about school.

Dad arranged for me to attend a different school that next fall. On the first day of class, it was tougher than I had expected. As I peered into all those unfamiliar faces, while walking down the foreign hallways, I felt uneasy and alone. It began to sink in that I knew no one; I was a nobody in my new surroundings. Anger began to boil up within me as I thought about the principal from my former school. It seemed he so effortlessly and uncaringly discarded me. I felt sorry for myself; but all that was about to change. I was surprised and thrilled, when a tall, blond guy stopped me and boldly introduced himself.

"Hey, I'm Bill. You're new here, aren't you?" His question had all the signs of genuine interest.

"Yeah," I said, "this is my first day—this place is different."

"Where are you from?" he asked.

I told Bill about being kicked out of my previous school, but left out the specific details. He only grinned.

"Where do you live?" Bill inquired.

When I answered, "Wycliffe subdivision," his eyes opened wide and he responded, "Me too. Let's walk home from school together this afternoon." We agreed on a place to meet in front of the school. As I walked away, I thought Bill just might turn out to be a good party buddy. That day, the school seemed so straight-laced to me. It was nestled in a quiet residential neighborhood and looked so homey. I figured the kids at this school weren't nearly as free and easy as the kids from my former school. How wrong I would be.

Moments after the final bell sounded that day, I met Bill outside. As we walked home, he told me about himself. He said he hated his parents, both of whom were alcoholics. They were affluent and successful, but he had no respect for them. His dad was a television announcer with one of our city's TV stations and was seldom around. Bill summed up his family situation by saying he lived in a house, not a home. I would soon learn he was not exaggerating.

That afternoon, Bill took a different route from the one I usually used. When I asked him where we were going, he shot back, "Just follow me." I could sense the nervousness in his voice. We went to the front door of a house that had great curb appeal. Bill rang the doorbell. While we waited for someone to answer, I asked, "What are you doing?" He glared at me impatiently and responded, "Shut up. Just pay attention." A cute teenage girl opened the door, and Bill simply stuck out his hand, fist clenched. She extended her hand toward him with an open palm, and he gave her some money. "Hold on," she said, and disappeared into the house. Within a few moments, she returned. Opening the door again, the girl handed Bill several joints, smiled, and said, "Thanks. Have a good time." Bill grabbed me by the arm and we jetted off. Passing through a wooded area, he said, "This is a good place." He took out one of the joints, lit it, and began to smoke, inhaling long and then holding it in longer than I had ever seen. I could tell he was studying my reaction. Savoring the first long toke, he said, "Hey, Jerry, you ever been high?"

"No," I said very slowly, yet deliberately.

"Here, hit on this," Bill said as he offered me the joint.

"I don't know." I was a bit hesitant.

"What do you mean, 'I don't know'? C'mon, Jerry, what are you going to do at the Friday and Saturday night parties if you say no?" His question intimidated me, but I just observed, nervously, as he finished.

We stopped by Bill's house, and I was invited in. When we walked into his bedroom, the scene shocked me. I couldn't help but be mesmerized by the giant note Bill had written on the wall. He had taken one of those huge smelly permanent markers and written an explicit message to his parents.

Dear Dad & Mom,

You -------. I hate your guts.

Why don't you go -------- on yourself?

Get out of my life. Go to hell.

Love, Bill

At home that night, I weighed the whole situation. Perhaps I could relate to Bill more than I was willing to admit. My mother was an alcoholic too, but it was the family secret. Everyone knew it, but we all acted oblivious to her problem and, in the end, we were all enablers. Every night, mom would retire early to her room, carrying a glass with vodka in it. I still remember hearing the ice clanging against the glass, as she walked past us in her robe, heading up to her bedroom. She went to bed drunk every night.

I was curious, and intrigued, with Bill's invitation to take that first hit of marijuana. Part of me wanted to say yes to drugs, but another part of me cried out, no! I wanted desperately to tell my dad about what had happened, about this new kid in my life, but I knew better. Dad would have totally freaked out. Confiding in him would have only resulted in another major fight. Unable to talk to my parents, that night I made the decision to try drugs at the next opportunity.

Three days later, Bill and I walked across the golf course to the house where my girlfriend, Laurie, lived. Laurie and I used to make out at night on the golf course, under the stars. My dad often referred to it as "spooning with the girls." But this day, we were there to see Laurie's sister, Michelle, who sold drugs—mainly pot. Bill bought a dime bag and took me behind some trees on the golf course. He reached into his pocket and took out a pipe. Putting a screen in it, he loaded the pipe with the dope. I took in every motion, from the striking of the match to the first hit. Then, the invitation for which I had been waiting, came again. Bill stuck the pipe in front of my lips and said, "C'mon. What are you waiting for?"

I coughed as that weed burned into my lungs for the first time. But with a few more tokes, I adjusted. I knew right then, that one time would not be enough. Soon, all I cared about was getting high. Before the bus picked me up, during school hours, immediately after school and always at the parties, I would smoke dope. That pipe became like a trusted friend. I carried the screen to it in my wallet, removing it whenever I had the chance to get a whiff of that can't-wait-until-next-time aroma.

Doing drugs was serious stuff for me and became a staple on weekends. My friends and I would usually go to someone's house for a let's-get-bombed party. The parents, of course, were somewhere else, having a party of their own, with their friends. Without supervision, there was nothing holding anyone back. Often, the goal was not simply pleasure, but performance. There was an obsession to outdo the previous week's experience.

One of the preferred things we did, was sit on the floor in a circle, light several joints, put them on roach clips, and pass them around and around. Then, we would try to hit on all of them at once. The goal was to see who could stay in the circle the longest. I can still see my friends and me getting high together and laughing incessantly at any comment that normally would not prompt a smile, let alone trigger a laugh.

Tragically, there was more than just marijuana. Somebody would bring alcohol and we would do drugs and drink—a dangerous combination. Everybody knew we were on the edge, but no one dared to say anything. And there were even worse things. One bizarre practice, popular in that era, was something called huffing. It involved mainly girls. To huff, a girl would lie flat on the floor while someone straddled her and held a hand towel tightly over her mouth. Another person would then spray an aerosol substance, through the towel, while the girl inhaled. It gave such a buzz, that some girls ended up acting crazy.

At nearly every party, sexual exploits were standard practice. In fact, some parties ended up with what (I know now) would later result in a lifetime of regrets. The party lifestyle continued for several months, and the goal for me became how many friends I could get to party with me. I got Bryan, Derek, and other kids into drugs. I wanted them to experience what I tricked myself into believing was incredible. Little did I realize, when I turned Sandy on to drugs at the bus stop, she would become an avid user and, several years later, would commit suicide. There are many motivating factors compelling me to reach as many young people as possible through my ministry—but there is no question—the memory of Sandy is a primary one.

At one wild party, on a cold spring night, I got high—really high. With my mind reeling, everything was blurred and amplified. Smoking dope can create a strong appetite we called the "munchies." So, I asked Bill to help me find something to eat. He came to my rescue and gave me a full plate of unbaked breakfast rolls and some other junk food. I quickly downed it all, without even realizing I was eating dough.

Just past midnight, Bill's dad picked us up. Sitting in the backseat of their car, I started coming down. My high was turning into a raunchy low. Mixing the drugs with all that junk food made me feel as if my insides were coming apart. Nauseated, I told Bill, "Man, I don't feel good," and I vomited all over the backseat. Bill's dad pulled curbside and the car came to a screeching halt, but even before it was fully stopped, Bill flung the door open and threw me out. I lay there on the grassy easement, stunned and sickened. The midnight chill enveloped me and, as I attempted to raise my body, my arms felt rubbery with weakness. I couldn't move. Bill's dad ordered him to pick me up. He thrust me back into the car for the remaining silent blocks to my house.

It took every ounce of energy for me to make

it to the front door. My parents were waiting up for me as I staggered in.

"What's wrong?" they asked.

"Nothing," I said indignantly.

"Are you sick, Jerry?"

"Just leave me alone." Refusing to even look at them, I pushed by and dragged myself up the stairs to my bedroom, which we affectionately called "the Big D." The title held no significance for me, or my brother Jeff, who shared this space with me.

The following morning, I felt no better. In fact, over the next few days, I became nauseated every time I ate. When I complained to my mom, she took me to our family doctor. He ran a battery of tests and discovered the source of my problem. I had a bleeding ulcer. The doctor had me hospitalized that same day. I am so glad I became physically sick; I think God used it to save my life.

Laid up in the depressing grayness of that hospital room, I ached with loneliness. The first ones to come and see me were some of my druggie friends, but they were not concerned about me as a person. One of them said, "Jerry, you have to get well so you won't miss out on the parties." I thought about that comment, and there, for the first time, it occurred to me there was nothing worth living for. You get high—you come down. It is an unending cycle. Drugs don't answer any questions or solve any problems. Instead, they just cloud them out temporarily and slowly weaken a person. Afterward, you are still empty, maybe even more so—unfulfilled, searching for something more.

Coming home from the hospital was a strange experience. I wanted things to be better, but I was doubtful they could be. I spent the next several weeks at home, attempting to recuperate. Concerned I would fall behind in my studies, my parents hired tutors to come to the house. Our family doctor prescribed Valium and sleeping pills to help me through the recovery period— the very items I would later use in an attempt to end my life. I carried those pill bottles with me constantly, in the deep pockets of my dad's light blue bathrobe. To me, they felt like a warm security blanket, but they were really an enemy in disguise. I lived in a drug-induced stupor. Already thin from the liquid diet I was on in the hospital, I eventually graduated to a bland diet and I lost even more weight. I did no exercise, nor did I want to. By the time I woke up each day, everyone in my family of seven was gone. I was left alone. Awful thoughts continued to plague me. Many times, I would hang my head and cry. Did anyone even care about what was happening to me? Did anyone notice? If I did away with myself, everyone would be better off, or so I reasoned. Who wanted to have a sick kid or brother moping around the house every day in his pajamas?

The days were long and, without having someone to talk to, depression and hopelessness quickly began to overpower me. Without me knowing, spring was in the air, and outside, everything was alive and blooming—but inside, I was withering and dying.

Standing in front of the television on that Friday, April 13, while reviewing the pictures of Mom and Dad and my brothers, I came to my own picture. *It wouldn't make any difference if you were gone.* The idea seemed so brilliantly simple. Reaching deep into the pocket of Dad's bathrobe, I wrapped my hands tightly around the bottles of pills. The voice in my head with rapid succession said, *"Kill yourself. Do it now. Take the pills and go to bed."* It was late morning. Surely I would be dead before anyone got home. I held the bottles more firmly, as if they were the best tickets to a big event and I was just about to enter the stadium.

Impulsively, I detoured and walked to the kitchen entryway and picked up the telephone receiver. Slowly, mechanically, I called my Dad's office. He answered in typical fashion.

"Johnston," he said gruffly. With tears flowing, I screamed my announcement, "Dad, this is Jerry. I'm going to kill myself."

His immediate response surprised me. I had finally taken the first step toward trusting my Dad for help—and his reaction was tender. This tough, workaholic father I had come to know, broke down at his desk. He began to weep over the phone, trying desperately to maintain control.

"Jerry, we'll do something. Son, please hold on. What can I do?"

"Nothing, Dad. It's all over. I'm sorry. My friends are gone. I'm sick. I'm all alone. I'm going to do it."

"Listen, Jerry, I'll be right there. Hold on. I'm coming home now!"

As a parent and grandfather now, I can only imagine the ride home for my dad that day. He later admitted to me that he cried and prayed the entire way, as he raced home, not sure in what condition he would find me.

Dad's office was downtown; driving the speed limit meant it would take him 30 minutes to get home, but on this morning, it seemed like only a few minutes. When Dad pulled in the driveway and raced into the house, I was lying on one of the beds, unstable and totally freaking out. Dad gently sat on the edge of the bed and, through tears, began reasoning with me. I reiterated over and over again, "Please, Dad, do something. Please, Dad; make this go away, please." For one hour he desperately tried his best to comfort me. When that failed, he finally said, "Jerry, let's go. I'm taking you to the hospital." Still wearing his big, light-blue bathrobe, I followed him as he gently led me to the car and rushed me to the emergency room of St. Luke's Hospital. To this very day, I can't remember the 15-minute ride there. I stayed at the hospital for over a week, enduring one test after another. The internists were stumped about my condition, since I showed no signs of improvement.

Easter Sunday morning, April 22, I was discharged from the hospital with a checkout weight of only 68 pounds. My parents guided me to the car in the beautiful sunlight, on that special Sunday. I peered out the window, on the ride home, contemplating what the future of my life would hold. Mom and Dad did their best to reassure me that everything was going to be okay. When we rounded the corner, pulling up to our house, there, waiting for me in the front yard, were my four brothers: Johnny, Jay, Jeff and Joel. Dad had everything prearranged. They were all on their best behavior, treating me as if I were a fragile vase. It was rather strange—such a bizarre contrast to memories of the five of us moving the furniture out of the living room when my parents would go out for the evenings and playing tackle football. We were all boys, and although we were rough and tough with each other, we all treated my mom rather gently, sort of the way they were all treating me now. Nobody wanted to say the wrong thing as, with my increasingly skinny body, I maneuvered my way out of the car, and up toward the front door. "Everything is going to be okay, Jerry!" one of my brothers announced.

How I wanted to believe those words. But inside, I was tormented with recurring thoughts of suicide. Like a pesky fly, the temptation kept buzzing around in my head. Frightened that I might go through with it, I wanted so much to blurt out to my parents the torturous thoughts with which I was still plagued. But I couldn't. Everyone was so happy to see me out of the hospital, and my bringing up something negative—let alone s-u-i-c-i-d-e—would ruin the artificial atmosphere. Dad was orchestrating everything as best he could. In his defense, what did he know about a kid wanting to kill himself? At that time, little was said or taught about recognizing suicidal behavior. Within a few years, America would start to record a surge in suicides among youth. My suicidal condition was early in the death-wish contagion that would later become so widespread. So, on that sunny Easter Sunday, with all the dark clouds and thoughts lurking in my mind, I played along.

I spent eleven long weeks, attempting to recuperate. Trapped inside our home, I felt like a mental and physical invalid. I became a hypochondriac. I just knew every day I was going to get sick and developed an extremely odd paranoia about vomiting. Those creepy thoughts of suicide were still there. I fought them by reminding myself that, someday soon, I'd be enjoying good times with my friends again.

While I struggled to fight my way back to normalcy, something sovereign and significant happened, though I did not realize it at the time. My brother, Johnny, became engaged to Teresa Barnes. Teresa was a refreshingly likable person, and the whole family was pleased with Johnny's choice. Politely, she invited our family to visit her church. Though we did not belong to that Christian denomination, and even though my dad initially resisted, for the sake of courtesy, we eventually attended with her.

For reasons I could not sort through, Teresa's church was different from our church. Though I was still feeling depressed and dejected, I sensed something compelling about the atmosphere there. Even from my seat on the back row, I somehow felt drawn in. One of the kids in the church's youth group spotted me and could read how confused and messed up I was. Without me knowing, a few of the courageous kids approached my dad and asked him if I could go with them to their upcoming annual summer youth camp. Their insistence caused something to click in him. Later that day, Dad approached me about the subject.

"Jerry, some of the kids at Teresa's church want you to go to summer camp with them in June." His tone was upbeat, but I could tell he was trying real hard to sound as if he wasn't putting something over on me.

"What kind of camp is it, Dad?" I asked, expressing no excitement.

"It's a Christian camp."

I thought my dad had gone crazy, suggesting something like that to me. "Are you kidding?" "You think I'm going to go for a week to some stupid monastery camp with a bunch of Jesus-freaks. No way!"

To me, a Christian was either a Boy Scout or a grandma. My dad knew I needed to go to that camp—for a lot of reasons. So he decided on a friendly, blackmail approach. With my birthday just a few days away, on May 12, he bought me an expensive gift and had it delivered to our basement without me knowing. When he came home later that day, he stopped me and said, "Jerry, I want you to change your mind about going to that camp."

"Drop it. Dad, I said no!"

He just smiled.

"I've got your birthday gift in the basement. Do you want to see it?"

Before I answered, I hurried down the basement stairs to discover what he had bought for me. I couldn't believe it! Right there, in my own home, was the most beautiful, professional foosball table I had ever seen. My friend, Bill, and I spent hours playing foosball, up at the arcade, competing against one another. My dad knew how much I enjoyed the game. I had already reached the table and was spinning the handles in anticipation of hours of fun when he dropped the bombshell.

"That's your birthday present…if you go to that camp. If not, I'll have it taken back."

I knew my dad well enough to realize he wasn't kidding. In the exhilaration of the moment, I reluctantly agreed.

In what seemed like the blink of an eye, on June 18, I found myself leaning against a station wagon in the parking lot of Teresa's church, getting ready for the drive down to Lake-of-the-Ozarks, Missouri, to a camp called Windermere. I felt really odd and out of place with those church kids. Hoping I wouldn't get sick on the three-hour drive, I grasped my pill bottles and managed to get into the right front passenger seat and sat, quiet and withdrawn, for the long drive.

The camp wasn't nearly as bad as I had predicted. I was surprised to discover there were a lot of interesting things to do. I was the loner, but without my knowledge, I had attracted the attention of some pretty cool looking older kids. Every night, they had a meeting in an auditorium, and I made sure to sit in the back row. It began with the kids singing some songs I had never heard, so I just silently watched while everybody sang. This routine went on for four days, and on the last night of camp, June 21, a very attractive girl named Cindy, walked from the front of the auditorium, all the way to the back row where I was parked, offered her hand and said, "Jerry, come sit with me. I want you to hear the message tonight." I wasn't so enthused about hearing the "message," but she was so gorgeous I could not refuse.

As I walked to the front of the auditorium, I'm sure I was quite a sight—long flowing blonde hair and my favorite jeans (which also served as my pajamas). I had had a girlfriend sew a large chicken claw patch on the rear of one of my back pockets. Everyone thought it was a marijuana patch. Some of the counselors looked as if they were going to have a heart attack when I took my seat on the second row.

I had fully planned to use the time to get more acquainted with Cindy. Instead, I experienced the greatest miracle of my life that night. The speaker spoke for an hour, and I was absolutely captivated. In a firm, powerful way, he told a story I had never heard. Because I listened to him and acted on his challenge, that night my life was revolutionized! I raced back to my cabin, grabbed my pill bottles and opened the lids on my way to the toilet. I watched as every one of them, individually, dropped into the water. Overjoyed, I flushed them away forever—and immediately felt renewed!

An upperclassman, who I had come to know, owned a cool sports car he had driven to camp that week. I was thrilled when he invited me to ride back home with him the next morning in his awesome Camaro. Like me, he too, had had a life change that week. We were both celebrating as we sped home. My parents almost passed out, when I burst through the front door and exclaimed, "Dad, Mom, I'm changed. I feel so good! Something happened at camp and I don't want to kill myself anymore. There is no more depression. I want to live!"

Their first reaction was, "Son, what are you up to now?" But, within moments, they broke down, crying, and have been shedding tears of joy ever since.

I returned home a radically different person. The confusion and craziness that had overpowered me was gone. I started to think straight. I started to live right. I began to grow, from that night on, in my understanding of what life is all about.

Later on, I will tell you what the camp speaker said that historic evening. But first, let's examine the subject of suicide. Together we will take a look at the causes, the misconceptions and the warning signs. And I will zero in on specific courses of action to help people who may be contemplating suicide.

CHAPTER 3

WARNING SIGNS

The most common health disorder is depression with over 25 percent (1 in 4) affected by mild symptoms. It is these young people that are at the highest risk for committing suicide.

"I can't believe it. She just wasn't the type of person you'd expect to commit suicide. There weren't any signs at all." I have lost count of the number of times I have heard parents say the same thing while telling me about the suicide of their child. The problem is, it is simply not true. Suicide is a problem, or set of problems (or motivated impulses), that develops with time, and ultimately erupts, generally after some type of trigger mechanism. Often, that trigger is some final disappointment, a state of perceived hopelessness that sends a person over the edge.

When a parent or grandparent says to me, "There was no indication of anything wrong. There was no clue as to a deep need, no sign of a serious problem," I must confess, I always raise my eyebrows in disbelief. Seldom does a teenager (or adult) commit suicide without giving some warning. My extensive research has borne this out. My conversations with many who have attempted suicide, and with family members and friends of a loved one who has completed suicide, reinforce this conviction. A spokesperson for the Suicide and Crisis Center in Dallas, says 80 percent of teenagers have given one or more signs of their intention beforehand. There *are* warning signs—deadly giveaways—that say a teenager is potentially suicidal. Knowing them can prevent a tragedy. But keep in mind that there is not one exclusive type of suicidal person, and different individuals will express the same warning signs differently. Some signs relate to what a person *does*; others to what a person *doesn't* do.

The following are a few signs for concern:

1. Withdrawal—The friend who pulls away. To a certain extent, withdrawal is natural and good during the teenage years. Developing healthy independence equips a teen for successful adulthood. But when withdrawal is severe, and there is an obvious pulling away into a shell, watch out.

Daily sensitivity is the key to recognizing

negative withdrawal. Unfortunately, our frenetic, contemporary lifestyle often desensitizes us. Social media can contribute to the isolation of a young person, particularly when he or she is depressed and has suicidal ideation. Without knowing it, we can find ourselves more interested in the families on TV shows, than in our own. One counselor points out that in some families, where a hectic pace is kept and family members do not pay much attention, withdrawal may not be noticed. In fact, in some families, far too often, withdrawal may even be welcomed.

Unwillingness to communicate is perhaps the most common form of withdrawal, but there are other telltale indicators. Failing grades can indicate a withdrawal from school. A broken romance can be a catalyst to withdrawal. The divorce of parents can cause kids to withdraw. Rejection of normally pleasurable activities, such as sports or hobbies, may suggest a self-punishing type of withdrawal. I know of students who made suicide attempts when they were cut from the varsity football or hockey team, the school play and other activities. An incessant desire to be alone, can also spell a disaster in the making. Make sure your friend is not pulling away, and if they are, notice it!

2. Moodiness—The friend who is up and down. Everyone is moody from time to time. We are all influenced by the weather, our health, circumstances and social relationships. Teenagers are no different.

But when there are wide shifts in personality and emotional make-up—up one day and rock-bottom the next—there is cause for concern and, possibly, alarm. One expert observed that sudden, inexplicable euphoria or whirlwind activity after a spell of gloom, means danger. There is ample evidence to conclude that many teens have ridden an emotional roller coaster to death. Let me give you an example: we have documented cases of youth suicide, where a teen, formerly withdrawn, becomes gregarious—unpredictably and artificially happy. It is a "live it up I am going to die soon" mentality. Conversely, we have also noted students who were formerly conversational, outgoing and engaging, who became silent and withdrawn. When the pendulum swings noticeably in a prominent, new and different direction for the person you know, take notice and do something. Moodiness is closely associated with the next two warning signs.

3. Depression—The friend who holds it

in. Depression is a highly individualized experience. Some teenagers, when they are depressed, become sullen and totally wrapped up in themselves. Others camouflage their feelings so well that no one is aware anything abnormal is happening. In such cases, the only way to find out what is happening, is by somehow getting the person to talk.

Health Canada reminds us of the key areas where a person can become depressed: the death or illness of someone close, difficulties at work or with a personal friendship, low self-esteem, financial difficulties and addictions.[1] The National Institute of Health Care Management in Washington, DC, reports that students with unidentified mental disorders are in poorer physical health and engage in more risky behaviors—like unsafe sexual activity, fighting and weapon carrying. The most common mental health disorder is depression, with over 25 percent (one in four) affected by mild symptoms. It is these young people who are at the highest risk for committing suicide.[2] Understanding how depression develops can be beneficial. Dr. Tim LaHaye theorizes it is nearly always the result of anger combined with self-pity. The anger may be due to a failure, an unrealized expectation, or a personal loss. As the emotions focus on whatever prompted the anger, feelings of self-pity follow.[3] Self-pity can give way to suicidal thoughts like, *"Nobody understands what I am going through,"* or *"There's no way I can get out of this situation."*

> **4. Aggression—*The friend who lashes out.*** Many suicide attempts are preceded by violent outbursts—fights, threats, cruel insults, even destruction of property. Frequently, acts of this nature are cries for help. But this kind of aggressive behavior, though usually out of character, often achieves the opposite result—rejection— rather than consideration. The teenager who wanted to be noticed, is condemned instead.

Look no further than the Aurora, Colorado, theatre massacre with James Holmes. He had been a PhD student in neuroscience at the University of Colorado, Anschutz Campus. Obviously, James knew he had a problem. Prior to the shooting, he met with not one, but at least three mental health professionals at the University of Colorado. They noticed something was off. Dr. Lynne Fenton, a psychiatrist at the school, was so concerned about Holmes' behavior, she contacted the university's threat assessment team nearly six weeks before

Holmes opened fire in a crowded theatre. Prosecutors claim Holmes "had conversations with a classmate about wanting to kill people in March, 2012, and (said) he would do so when his life was over." [4] Nothing was done in time to intervene in Holmes' maniacal condition.

Dylan Klebold, one of the killers in the Columbine high school shooting wrote in his diary, "People are so unaware…well, ignorance is bliss, I guess…that would explain my depression."[5] His sad diary continues, "I don't fit in. I've been thinking of suicide…no hope that I'll be in my place wherever I go after this life… that I'll finally not be at war with myself, the world, the universe—my mind, body." Helped by his accomplice, Eric Harris, this depressed duo killed 12 students and injured 24 others, before taking their own lives. As a parent, would you not demand to see the school paper your son had written about a mass murder? I have a hard time accepting the gullibility of Sue Harris, Dylan's mom, who, 10 years later, wrote in O Magazine:

> "These thoughts may seem foolish in light of what we know now, but they reflect what we believed to be true about Dylan. Yes, he had filled notebook pages with his private thoughts and feelings, repeatedly

expressing profound alienation. But we'd never seen those notebooks. And, yes, he'd written a school paper about a man in a black trench coat who brutally murders nine students. But we'd never seen the paper. (Although it had alarmed his English teacher enough to bring it to our attention, when we asked to see the paper at a parent-teacher conference, she didn't have it with her…we agreed that she would show the paper to Dylan's guidance counselor; if he thought it was a problem, one of them would contact me. I never heard from them.)" [6]

Respectfully, I don't buy it. If your son had written an essay about killing nine classmates at school, would you not have demanded to see the paper? In the same article, Mrs. Klebold says after the Columbine murders, she started to learn all she could about suicide. That is good, but it is too late. In the infamous "basement tapes," both Klebold and Harris record and boast about concocting their plan under the noses of their unsuspecting parents and friends. On the tapes, Dylan refers to the teenager Rachel Scott, who he gunned down just outside the school, as a "godly little whore."[7] Harris kept the shotgun he used in the killings in the closet in his bedroom.

These troubled friends planned this massacre for months.

A less obvious form of pre-suicidal aggression is risk-taking. This could include recklessness with cars or participation in dangerous activities. An 18-year-old boasted that a death wish motivated him to take up skydiving and wing walking on airplanes. In counseling, it was discovered he was trying to get the attention of his father, who ignored him.

> **5. Alcohol and drug abuse—*The friend who starts using.*** Alcohol and drugs are always an escape, but especially for the person with life-ending thoughts. Sudden indulgence by a young person with no history of abusing alcohol or experimenting with drugs is a definite red flag.

> **6. Sexual activity—*The friend who lets go.*** Inappropriate sexual behavior sometimes reflects a desperate desire to relieve depression. By letting go completely with another person, the depressed teenager thinks satisfaction can finally be achieved. When there is no lasting satisfaction, suicidal thoughts can, and often do, intensify.

> **7. Eating disorders—*The friend who***

punishes himself or herself. Anorexia and bulimia are words now well known in North America. These frightful diseases have a strong connection to self-destructive thoughts and should always be considered as potential indicators of death wishes. Concerned friends and family members should watch for drastic weight loss.

8. Gift giving—*The friend who gives up and gives away.* Some young people who plan to take their lives will give away prized possessions to close friends, or to others who they wish were close friends. Suicide experts say this is an ominous action; a silver cloud with a very dark lining. It should prompt serious, concerned questioning. I have had parents of children who committed suicide tell me that in retrospect, they should have known. It was so obvious and well-planned. Regretfully, their awareness came too late.

9. Trauma—*The friend who's been hit hard.* Each person has an emotional threshold, an internal breaking point. A major traumatic event or series of circumstances can drive a teenager closer and closer to that edge. A family's move to another community can seem like the end of the world to a young person who has built strong ties and sunk deep roots. The trauma of a divorce, a death or an accident—any such experience can hit a friend hard—leaving the young person stunned, with thoughts of suicide running unbridled. And remember, one of the most significant traumas a teenager can experience is the suicide of a friend or family member. Suicidologists refer to this phenomenon as a *contagion affect*. Rarely do we hear of just one teen suicide in a school, community, or multigenerational family when a person commits suicide. To a close friend or family member, it can induce not only feelings of guilt and sorrow, but elevate personal problems to a perceived abnormal level. In North America, we have experienced scores of communities that registered as suicide clusters. A few decades ago, the media would play up adolescent suicides and it had a tragic, perpetuating effect. The U.S. government made recommendations to media to discourage the emotional retelling of youth suicides and there has been a notable change in media coverage, but youth suicide still occurs at alarming levels.

In both the United States and Canada, it is on the rise—but the in-depth, personal stories are seldom written anymore (unless the story involves celebrities). Responsible journalism factors in the potential suicides waiting to happen and exercises restraint and responsibility.

10. Personality change—The friend who's not the same. Abrupt reversal is the thing to watch for. When a usually introverted person suddenly begins to act like an unbridled extrovert, joking and carrying on, it's not necessarily a laughing matter. Conversely, this holds true when the gregarious person becomes a silent loner. Personality change can be expressed in a lowered energy level, neglect of responsibility, elimination of personal ambition or an I-don't-care attitude toward personal appearance. Don't be afraid to intervene when you see these noticeable personality changes.

11. Threat—The friend who speaks out. Any comment regarding the desire to die should always be taken seriously. Some of the most common threats are, "I wish I'd never been born," or, "You're going to be sorry when I'm gone," or, "I want to go to sleep and never wake up." These threats should be interpreted as seriously as, "I'm going to kill myself."

As I have mentioned repeatedly, be diligent in watching for these signs. Don't feel helpless, because you're not. You can help a suicidal person. You must communicate openly with the person, asking questions to probe the troubled individual's thoughts. You must empathize, not being judgmental or harsh, but not being overly sympathetic either. And you *must* act! In the following pages I will give more specific guidelines on what you can do.

CHAPTER 4

COMMON MYTHS ABOUT SUICIDE

The exponential impact on the immediate family and friends of each person who commits suicide, reveals that this traumatizes thousands of people each year.

Worldwide, 1,000,000 people take their lives each year—a staggering number! Every 15 minutes, someone commits suicide in the United States. More U.S. citizens kill themselves than kill one another, every year! In fact, there are twice as many suicides as murders. One in five suicides in the United States is a war veteran. Native American/Alaska Native youth have the highest rate of suicide, with 14.8 suicides per 100,000. White youth are next highest, with 7.3 deaths per 100,000. Males take their lives at nearly five times the rate of females and represent more than 80 percent of all U.S. suicides.[8] Women, however, during their lifetime, attempt suicide about two to three times more often than men.

In a recent interview, Dr. Alex Crosby, foremost expert on youth suicide and medical epidemiologist at the Centers for Disease Control in Atlanta, Georgia, shared, with me, that the growing trend is for young females to commit suicide by hanging. It is something of a mystery the CDC is studying. We spent an hour discussing the realities and implications of teen suicide.

Suicide rates for females are highest among those aged 45-54 and there is an increased number of suicides among middle age men. At the present time, poisoning is the most common method of suicide for females. Firearms are most commonly used by males.[9] Suicide is the second-leading cause of death among college students, and the third-leading cause of death among those aged 15-24 years. It is the fourth-leading cause of death among those aged 10-14 years.[10] We would refer to these deaths as completed suicides; for every person who takes his or her life, there are 25 attempted suicides.[11] The National Institute of Mental Health documents a six-year-old who killed himself! The exponential impact on the immediate family and friends of each person who commits suicide, reveals that this traumatizes thousands of people each year. Suicide is the second leading cause of death among teenagers in Canada. Experts warn that the beginning of the school term is a perilous time. As in the United States, in Canada, more young men complete suicide; but four times as many Canadian young girls attempt suicide. Shockingly, Canada's youth-suicide rate, per capita, is nearly triple that of the United States. In part, this is explained by the high suicide rates in the Canadian native communities. The age-standardized mortality rate in Nunavut, the fifth-largest country subdivision in the world and a major part of Northern Canada, is the highest in Canada at 51.2 suicides per 100,000 people; a rate that is 3-6 times higher than the rate in other provinces/territories. The suicide rate in males is over four-and-a-half times the rate of females.[12] The number of girls committing suicide in Canada has risen in the past 30 years; a troubling trend that is prompting some experts to question the interplay of social media. Another concerning shift, is the *way* young people are killing themselves. Researchers noted a decrease in suicide from poisoning or firearms. According to a study published in the 2012 Canadian Medical Association Journal, which used data from the Public Health Agency of Canada, suffocation, which includes hanging and strangulation, is now the predominant method of suicide among children and adolescents. Statistics Canada reports hangings have been the most common method of suicide since 1992, but it was used less often at older ages.[13] And, as studies have proven in other areas, marriage is a deterrent to suicide. In general, married people were the least likely to commit suicide, as compared with single, widowed or divorced individuals.

A young man named Tony stood next to me, at one of our events, and asked that I read a statement to the few thousand teens who had assembled in the auditorium. The reason I was reading his thought-provoking words, was because, in his attempt to kill himself with a gun, Tony had blown most of his face, literally, off his head. His girlfriend, Missy, had heard me speak in her public school and told me about his horrific situation. I followed up and went to see him. We developed a friendship of trust. In his suicide attempt, the gunshot had blown off Tony's nose, most of his face under his eyes, his mandible bone and the majority of his teeth. Plastic surgeons had formed two slits for air holes, in replacement of his nose, so he could breathe and close most of his mouth. Tony was fed directly into his stomach. He was a frightful sight.

This is the other side of suicide: most young people, who romanticize with suicidal ideation, rarely think about the consequences of a failed attempt. Only after impairing himself so dramatically did Tony realize what a priceless gift life truly is. He wants to live now, more than ever, and faces years of excruciatingly painful surgeries, in hopes of looking human again. You can imagine how frozen that youth audience was as I read Tony's words, telling them to stay off drugs and make wise decisions—as his stare penetrated the audience.

Candidly, it is not that easy to kill yourself. Imagine being depressed and suicidal, making the attempt, and then waking up to find out you are paralyzed; can't speak, walk or see. It happens innumerable times every year. People become prisoners within their inoperable bodies.

We now hear of "psychological autopsies." Tragically and belatedly, parents, counselors, psychiatrists and mental health experts work to put together a composite of the emotional and psychological disorders of someone who has completed suicide. But, in a sense, it is too late —the data can help only with *other* potential victims.

Social media makes it easier than ever for

young people to share their thoughts and connect with others, which isn't always a positive thing. Cyber bullying has become a serious problem across North America. There are countless websites where users can share suicidal thoughts, and even instructions on methods to kill themselves.

People who see a serious bullying problem should talk to school authorities. More and more states are implementing laws against bullying. Recent lawsuits against schools and criminal charges against bullies show there are legal avenues to deal with bullies. If school authorities do not help with an ongoing bullying problem, local police or attorneys will be able to do so.

Before you finish reading this chapter, several teenagers throughout North America will try to kill themselves. Just one life lost is one too many. The deaths will make news for a day, and then be forgotten by the public. Family, friends and acquaintances will be left in the aftermath, groping through a dense fog of uncertainty. They will wonder, evaluate and ask time and again, "Why did they die? Why did they commit suicide?" The unknown will lead to speculation, and the speculation will lead to wrong conclusions. I say this with certainty, because I have seen it happen so frequently. Misconceptions about suicide are prevalent.

Many people are hesitant to even discuss the subject of suicide. I distinctly remember teachers, principals, pastors and priests, who feared that if I were to talk about suicide, it would cause people to take their lives. Nothing could be further from the truth, as every suicidologist and mental health worker knows. Thankfully, much of that ignorant attitude has dissipated across North America, but more work needs to be done to eliminate the common myths about suicide.

I am convinced most of our statistics regarding suicide (at least in the United States) are inaccurate. Follow my argument. As we are aware, there is a certain amount of death certificate error and bias with some suicides. The statistics collected and reported by the Centre for Disease Control (CDC) are from indisputably recognized suicides. Ironically, many alcohol and drug-related deaths are not certified as suicides and are therefore not in our totals. Also, we know some affluent families want to avoid the stigma of suicide and this, too, influences the registry at death. In addition, there are theological implications, for some faiths, if a person commits suicide. In certain faith systems, it equates to instant damnation. This bias influences "cause of death" on the cases where it is not an indisputably recognized suicide, and sometimes, even if it is. The collecting of data from coroners across the country is not always efficient and comprehensive. Every case of morbidity, which finds its way in to the sorting categories of death registered at the CDC is highly doubtful. What about the accuracy of rural America? What about the thousands of missing persons in the U.S.? How many alcohol-related crashes were disguised suicides? How many drug-induced deaths were those of people who simply had lost the will to live? And, what of the multiplied thousands of family members and close friends who develop mental and emotional problems, and even experience early death, from grieving over the suicide of someone they loved? Perhaps Canada has a much more comprehensive support system, due to its population, than the United States. If you think the numbers of suicides are alarming, and indeed they are, I think we would be shocked if we knew the actual numbers of people who are committing suicide annually—a much higher number indeed.

Most people have some misconceptions about suicide. I know I did. So, once and for all, let's set the record straight on several key points. Let's dispel some commonly held myths about suicide.

Myth #1—People who talk about suicide don't commit suicide. Wrong. Dead wrong. Dr. Edwin Schneidman, respected for his knowledge in the field, reminds us that the notion people who talk about suicide don't do it, is the most dangerous myth in the world. Four out of five people who complete suicide have made previous attempts, and in every single instance, there were clues and warning signals.

What if a suicidal person dares to talk to you about self-destructive thoughts? How will you respond? Many people, often parents in particular, out of fear and ignorance, hesitate or refuse to get involved. Wrongly, they think by discussing the issue with the suicidal person, the risk will heighten. Not so. By expressing their morbid thoughts, the suicidal person is saying, "Help me! I'm trying to get a handle on this!"

Let me give you a strategy of compassion, concern, and intervention. If someone you know is exhibiting any of the warning signs of suicidal ideation, I recommend the following:

- *Listen and observe the person very carefully.* Don't do all the talking; and certainly don't preach at a hurting person.

Emotions are raw when a person is suicidal. Think of how gently you would respond to someone if he or she had a broken arm, wrist or leg. Now approach the person emotionally with the same care, quietness and attentiveness. Invite the suicidal person to explain to you what is bothering him or her. Be aware he or she may not have the ability to articulate the problem(s). You're not dealing with a used car salesman. Let the person talk. Look into his or her eyes. Stay quiet and listen. Remember, too, when a teenager is abusing drugs or alcohol, he or she is communicating through the behavior. Someone abusing drugs and alcohol is telling you, "I am in pain. I have to medicate myself because I am hurting." For you to simply watch their addiction grow more severe, year after year, makes you an enabler of the worst kind. My mother was alcoholic my entire childhood. She never said she wanted to kill herself, but she was drinking herself to death. I knew she was going to die if my four brothers and I did not do something about her degenerating condition. To make a long story short, one prearranged night, my brothers (with me serving as the ringleader), arrived, unannounced, at my parents home, picked up my mom physically and took her to a local hospital. We checked her in against her will. I remember how angry she was at me! Our drastic action literally saved her life. Mom has been alcohol-free for nearly 25 years. I tell parents, "Don't tell me you love your son or daughter, when you know they are doing drugs or alcohol, or hanging out with the wrong people and you do nothing about it." That is not love. That is being an enabler. People who are suicidal are depending upon us to notice, care and do something about their troubled condition! Listen, listen, listen and keep listening.

- *Identify with the hurting person.* If your friend tells you they have been thinking about ending their life, don't look at them as though they are some kind of freak. Identify with the hurting person. Suicidologists remind us that most people, at some point in their lives, have had a fleeting (to serious) thought about ending their lives. Admit it. I told you my story in this book. Since the time when I was a teenager, I have faced a number of particularly challenging days, when I did not think I could go on. I loved God. I loved my wife Cristie. I loved my three kids and their spouses. I loved my grandchildren. Simultaneously, I was simply overwhelmed. It's called life. And, thankfully, I have had three key people, in my life, who have always been there to listen and observe me carefully.

- *Initiate a loving, calculated response (Be very, very careful).* Here is a hypothetical conversation between a father (we will call Sam) and his 17-year-old son, Kelly, who has been morose and dejected. Sam knows his kid is in trouble. He has pillow-talked the concern for his boy to his wife, night after night. Sam could approach his son like this: "Kelly, you have been acting as though you have been down lately—are you?" (Wait for a response.) "Kelly, did you know your dad has had times in his life when he has been depressed, too? In fact, Kelly, there were times I did not know if I could go on. Are you having similar thoughts?"

- *Ask the key question.* Whenever we suspect someone near and dear to us is contemplating taking his or her life, there is an essential question that must be asked. *Do you have a plan or method to take your life? Have you considered an actual time to do it?* Whenever a person has logically thought out a plan or method to commit suicide, and associated a specific timetable to it, he or she is in immediate danger and should never be left alone. You must get that suicidal person to a trained professional who has expertise in diagnosing the situation and making specific recommendations for help and healing. This may require hospitalization; or the expertise of a reputable counselor, psychiatrist, or trained, experienced pastor who can intervene. Don't get in over your head; seek help from someone truly qualified. Take a look in the back of this book—one of the most effective suicide hotlines is **1-800-273-TALK (8255)**. There also may be a local suicide hotline in your area. I have had counseling experiences with young people where I would not end the session without privately calling the adolescent's parents and telling them I was convinced their child was at high risk and needed to be hospitalized. I've been engaged in this work long enough to know, there is no room for error. On one occasion, I happened to make a house call, and after repeated knocks on the door, no one came to answer. Yet, through the window, I could see the teen I had come to see, sleeping peacefully on the couch in the living room. It didn't make sense. I was making enough noise to easily wake him up and yet he did not move. Something compelled me to crawl through an unlocked window into the home, where I discovered the young man had taken 36 Quaaludes and was almost dead! I rode in the ambulance and watched, with the greatest grief, as paramedics feverishly pumped the boy's stomach on the way to the hospital. Miraculously, he lived. What if I had left that front door and assumed he was just in a deep sleep? Don't be afraid to intervene when you know someone is crying out for help.

Myth #2—Suicides usually happen without warning. No, suicides do not occur unpredictably. They are, more often than not, the result of a long-term inner struggle, that is expressed outwardly in some clearly recognizable actions and attitudes. There is almost always a clue, usually several, that a person is suicidal. A suicidal person shows signs of depression, like ongoing sadness, withdrawal from others, losing interest in favorite activities, or trouble sleeping or eating. It is not uncommon to notice a preoccupation with death, or death themes, and an interest in dying. The engagement in deliberately dangerous or harmful activities; including reckless behavior, substance abuse, or self-injury can be seen as warnings. Frequent expressions like, "I can't handle this any more," or "I am so tired of living," should be taken as verbal warnings. A suicidal person often exhibits:

- Feelings of hopelessness or worthlessness, depression and low self esteem or guilt

- Lack of desire to participate in family or social activities in which he or she participated previously

- A marked change in sleeping or eating patterns

- Feelings of rage, anger, or a need for revenge

- Lack of energy; lethargy

- Poor academic performance; desire to quit a job or school

- Multiple emotional outbursts, or apparent absence of emotion

- Lack of hygiene and self care

- Excessive abuse of drugs or alcohol

- Sexual promiscuity or lack of interest in sex

- Comments on physical symptoms of discomfort

Myth #3—Suicidal people can't be talked out of it if they are really intent on dying. Dr. Schneidman again provides direction, saying, "Nonsense! [A suicidal person] is in a state of confusion and irrational thinking; he wants to continue his life but can't see the way. We find, so frequently, that lethal drives last just a short time, so that if you can get him through the period of severe stress, his entire outlook can change and the very next day he may no longer be the slightest bit suicidal."[14]

Nearly every suicidal person is torn between living and dying, to such an extent that one authority says the leap off a building may be the tragic result of a 51 to 49 internal vote. For concerned friends, this wavering between two sides is an opportunity to speak up and reach out.

Myth #4—An individual's improvement, following a suicidal crisis, means the suicide risk is over. A young man named Paul, tried to hang himself because, as he put it in a terse note to his parents:

Nobody loves me. Nobody really talks to me. They just throw words at me.

Paul survived, however, and seemed to be making improvement. "I thought he had solved his problem," said his father. But Paul made a second attempt, four months after the first. Help arrived too late. His final note read:

Nobody listens. They say, "How are you?" and that's about as far as it goes. I don't want to live in a world where it hurts so bad inside all the time.

Paul's case, unfortunately, is tragically typical. The person most likely to complete suicide, is one who failed in a previous attempt. Of all the signs, this one is the most foreboding. The parent or friend's role in this circumstance is to act, not assume. Saying, "I thought he was getting better," will not bring the person back. After a failed attempt, it is imperative to show you care, by spending time, daily, with the person; talking, doing things together, enjoying life and insuring that the person who has attempted suicide is regularly being counseled by someone qualified, i.e., a mental health therapist, a trained counselor or an experienced pastor.

Myth #5—Suicide strikes more often among

the rich. I like what N. L. Farberow says about this: "Suicide is neither the rich man's disease, nor the poor man's curse."[15] In fact, suicide is very democratic and includes a proportionate number of victims from all levels of society. Another study indicates that the average person who commits suicide is close to the average person.

Myth #6—Suicide is hereditary; it runs in families. There is absolutely no evidence to suggest suicidal tendencies are hereditary. We do know some mental illnesses are multigenerational, and we can assuredly attribute some suicides to mental illness. Also, there is, unquestionably, a powerful negative influence on surviving families when a suicide occurs. One psychiatrist calls it survivor's guilt—a curious belief that the "wrong person" died. A confused teenager told me, "My father was such a good man. He never hurt anybody and worked so hard for the family. Look at me. I'm a mess, and I keep screwing up in everything I do. Why am I the one still alive?"

When a family member takes his or her own life, it can prompt suicidal thoughts, and even a suicide attempt among the survivors. This is especially true of a survivor who is already deeply troubled. But none of this has anything to do with genetic factors. No one is doomed to act a certain way, or destined to end it all because a family member made a fateful decision.

Myth #7—Someone who commits suicide is mentally ill. Marcia attempted suicide when she was 15 and again at 17. In her own words, she told why:

> The agony and the confusion at the time seemed permanent. My main concern was, that if the situation I was in was going to be permanent, I wanted no part of it. That death would be permanent, was of no consideration to me. There is a great feeling of being hopeless and lost, and your self-image is in pretty bad shape when you're thinking about suicide.

Marcia, I am convinced, is not mentally ill. She is quite normal and, thankfully, quite alive today. But she does illustrate the severity of adjustment during the teenage years. Like the butterfly freeing itself from the cocoon, the teenager must stretch new emotional muscles before finally breaking. It is a wonderful, difficult time, and there are many obstacles along the way. Kids tell me about their pain, their feelings of rejection, and the ugly suspicion that no one really cares. But they are not insane. Let me say, there are mental illnesses which contribute to completed suicides, but not all people who complete suicide are mentally ill. I am aware some psychiatrists might debate me on this point. It has been my observation, that people who are not mentally ill, and have had no history of mental illness, have made suicide attempts, or completed suicide, due to the problems and complications in their lives.

Some very bright young people take their lives because they no longer want to mask the secret torment that lurks inside. A prominent medical journal reported its finding that 12 percent of grade-school children, age six to twelve years, have had suicidal ideas or made suicidal threats. Are these children crazy? No. Are they vulnerable? You better believe they are.

Myth #8—Only young people commit suicide in significant numbers. Suicide is the third-leading cause of death for U.S. teenagers, and the second leading cause of death for Canadian teens. However, older Americans are disproportionately more likely to die by suicide. Of every 100,000 people, ages 65 and older, 14.3 died by suicide in 2007 in the U.S. This figure is higher than the national average of 11.3 suicides per 100,000 people in the general population.[16]

Myth #9—Women threaten suicide, but

men carry it out. This myth comes from a misinterpreted fact. As stated earlier, five times as many men as women *complete* suicide, but two to three times as many women *attempt* suicide. The explanation for this phenomenon lies in the suicide method. Historically, women choose less violent methods, such as pills or poison, increasing the chance of rescue. When I asked Dr. Crosby at the CDC why there is a slow reversal of this trend with more adolescent girls choosing hanging, he answered, "We're not sure." The CDC continues to probe this mystery, as with many other mysterious aspects of suicide.

Myth #10—Talking about suicide causes it, by planting the idea in a person's head. I am amazed at how widespread this myth really is! In years past, I have had some critics claim I inadvertently encourage teenagers to commit suicide by addressing the topic. Every suicidologist will adamantly deny, that by talking about suicide, or confronting individuals who have a suicidal ideation, it causes suicides. The opposite is true. I know many young people are already thinking about suicide, and they are often convinced no one has ever felt the way they do, or cared about the way they feel. By talking about suicide, and by identifying causal reasons and the feelings they are experiencing, we are bringing everything out in the open. Just knowing that others are struggling too, helps immeasurably, in a teenager's ability to cope. No, talking about suicide will not cause suicide. But failing to talk about it may have disastrous consequences.

Now, let's take a little test:

- Talking about suicide will plant the idea in a depressed person's mind. True/**False**

- People who talk about suicide usually do not follow through with it. True/**False**

- Most suicides occur without warning. True/**False**

- If there is no note, it was not a suicide. True/**False**

- When depression lifts, suicide is no longer a concern. True/**False**

- A suicidal person cannot be talked out of it if he/she is intent on dying. True/**False**

- Women threaten suicide, but only men complete suicide. True/**False**

- Only certain people are the suicidal type. True/**False**

- African American men complete suicide in the same numbers as Caucasian men.

True/**False**

- Only insane or "crazy" people complete suicide. True/**False**

- If a person has survived a suicide attempt, the likelihood of a second attempt is diminished. True/**False**

- People who complete suicide have not sought medical help prior to the attempt. True/**False**

CHAPTER 5
‖‖‖‖‖‖‖‖‖‖‖‖‖‖‖‖‖‖‖‖‖‖‖‖‖‖‖‖‖‖‖‖‖

THE BULLYING OF AMANDA TODD

"I have nobody. I need someone."

Over thirteen million people have watched the YouTube video of Amanda Todd, posted on September 7, 2012, from Coquitlam, British Columbia. Amanda committed suicide on October 10th, less than one month before her birthday, at age 15, after months of bullying. Her video was a cry for help and reflects the sad reality of what is happening all over North America, and even around the world. Amanda, expressed her suicide intent pitifully, as she successively held little cards that piecemealed her story. The following is an unedited version, just as Amanda wrote on her cards.

Hello ...

I've decided to tell you about my never ending story. In 7th grade I would go with friends on webcam. Meet and talk to new people. Then got

called stunning, beautiful, perfect, etc ...
Then wanted me to flash ... So I did ...
1 year later ... I got a msg on facebook
From him ...

Don't know how he knew me ... It
said ... If you don't put on a show
for me I will send ur boobs. He knew
my address, school, relatives, friends,
family names. Christmas break ...
Knock at my door at 4 am ... It was
the police ... my photo was sent to
everyone. I then got really sick and got
...Anxiety, major depression and panic
disorder. I then moved and got into
Drugs & Alcohol ...

My anxiety got worse ... couldn't go
out. A year past and the guy came back
with my new list of friends and school.
But made a facebook page. My boobs
were his profile pic. Cried every night,
lost all my friends and respect people
had for me ... again ... Then nobody liked
me, name calling, judged ... I can never
get that Photo back. It's out there
forever ...

I start cutting ... I promised myself
never again ... Didn't have any friends and
I sat at lunch alone. So I moved

Schools again ... Everything was better even though I sat still alone at lunch in the library everday.

After a month later I started talking to an old guy friend. We back and fourth texted and he started to say he liked me ... led me on. He had a girlfriend. then he said come over my gf's on vacation.

So I did ... huge mistake ... He hooked up with me ... I thought he liked me ...

1 week later I got a text get out of your school. His girlfriend and 15 others came including himself ... The girl and 2 others just said look around nobody likes you in front of my new school (50) people. A guy than yelled just punch her already. So she did. She threw me to the ground and punched me several times. Kids filmed it. I was all alone and left on the ground. I felt like a joke in this world ... I thought nobody deserves this :/.

I was alone ... I lied and said it was my fault and my idea. I didn't want him getting hurt, I thought he really liked me but he just wanted the sex ... Someone yelled punch her already. Teachers ran over but I just went and layed in a ditch and my dad found me. I wanted to die so bad

... when he brought me home ... I drank bleach ... It killed me inside and I thought I was gonna actually die. Ambulence came and brought me to the hospital and flushed me. After I got home all I saw was on facebook - she deserved it, did you wash the mud out of your hair? I hope she's dead. Nobody cared ...

I moved away to another city to my moms. Another school ... I didn't wanna press charges because I wanted to move on.

6 months has gone by ... people are posting pics of bleach, clorex and ditches ... tagging me ... I was doing a lot better too ... they said ... She should try a different bleach. I hope she dies this time and isn't so stupid. Why do I get this? I messed up but why follow me? I left your guys city...

I'm constantly crying now ... Everyday I think why am I still here? My anxiety is horrible now. Never went out this *summer. All from my past ... lifes never getting better ... cant go to school*

Meet or be with people ... constantly cutting. Im really depressed. I'm on anti deppresants now and councelling and a month ago this summer I overdosed ... in hospital for 2 days ...

Im stuck

Whats left of me now ... nothing stops. I have nobody ... I need someone. My name is Amanda Todd.

Amanda's story makes you heartsick. At 12, she was enticed by a cyberstalker to flash her body online. The stalker, as you read, haunted her for years until her self-inflicted death. Other kids tormented her and called her a "porn star." British Columbia has pledged $2 million for new prevention initiatives, and even has an "Anti-Bullying Day." Legislation can go only so far. The best protection is the close, constant support, supervision, and, if need be, intervention of parents. My message to kids is simple: if you are being bullied, tell your parents, tell the school counselor, even the police.

Thank God, Facebook has launched a bold, anti-bullying campaign. Nearly every piece of content on Facebook has a report link. So, if someone is hassling or threatening you—report them. Don't be silent. Find someone you trust and talk to them. Don't cover for an alleged boyfriend or girlfriend regardless of what interaction you have had with them. I ask every teenager to remember:

1. You don't deserve to be bullied, regardless of what you have done. Do *not* permit yourself to become a victim for anyone. Every person deserves to be treated with respect.

2. Do not post any personal pictures of yourself on the Internet. Everything on the Internet lives forever, and can—and will—be used against you. Use discretion. Put your camera down and use utmost discretion when the webcam is on.

3. Start a "Be Nice" campaign in your school and social network. Get ahead of the rude and insulting behavior of people who want to be show-offs, by initiating a "respect movement" in your school. Ask for the school and its leadership to back you up and bring some real "teeth" to respond quickly to offenders.

4. Remember—you do not secure a boyfriend or girlfriend by surrendering to coercion and manipulation. Respect yourself. Don't hesitate to stand up for your values and tell any friend or supposed boyfriend or girlfriend to leave you alone if they are trying to threaten you.

5. Turn in the offender. Consensus rises against mean people when nice people won't put up with their offensive, rude behavior. Speak up and don't tolerate it.

For parents—pay attention! If your child's eating or sleeping habits change, it could signal they are being bullied. A student's grades going south, a loss of interest in school activities, and your child, morphing into a loner, are clear telltale signs. Read the signals and care enough to ask, "Is someone bothering you? Are you being threatened?" Amanda's YouTube video included a picture of her wrists repeatedly scarred with dried blood where she had been cutting. I don't know why her parents didn't notice. My message to parents is: take the time to notice everything—any hint could be a clue and a cause for intervention.

CHAPTER 6

HOW TO RESCUE YOUR FRIEND

"Looking back, I realize I was not there when he needed me."

What if I were to tell you one of my early pastors killed himself? He was a man you would never have expected to die by suicide; a brilliant, gifted teacher and speaker, with friends all over America. I remember his tremendous messages. In the early years of my career, he and his wife befriended my wife, Cristie, and me. We developed a custom of picking a nice restaurant, taking turns at hosting one another for a delicious meal and spending hours talking. I vividly remember those wonderful nights of fellowship. We would stay for hours, opening our hearts with one another and sharing the progress we were making. Some nights, we dined until the restaurant was ready to turn out the lights, forcing us to go home.

His wife was a dear lady who was rather quiet.

When she did interject a thought, it was always caring and reflected her kind heart. Over a period of months, both Cristie and I noticed he was a bit sharp with his wife. It was not uncommon for him to cut her off, mid-sentence, or correct something she had said. To us, it came across in a demeaning manner. It was a little embarrassing, and we felt bad for her. In a sense, he treated her more as though she was his child than his wife.

I held a number of conferences in his church that attracted thousands of people. I remember the many nights we would entertain some of the most celebrated communicators in America together. He was great fun and had great opinions and ideas on a myriad of subjects. I remember one night, when I was going through a stressful time, he called and gave me great comfort and encouragement.

After a long career in one city, he received an invitation to become pastor of one of the largest churches in America. After careful consideration, he accepted. The next time we were together was one Sunday morning, when I spoke for him in his new, 4,000 seat church. I remember, as if it was yesterday, him leaning over and whispering in my ear, "Jerry, do you see why I took this church?" I didn't have the heart to respond and tell him what I was really thinking. The church seemed something of an antique to me, stuck in the past.

In his new position, my friend became very egocentric. Frequently, he would boast about how much the church was paying him or the interest-free, $100,000 line-of-credit, he had successfully secured, should he need it at any time. On the way home, Cristie and I commented to one another that he seemed to have changed. We remembered back to those early dinners when he shed tears and opened his heart to us about both the joys and regrets of ministry. That was the man with whom we had fallen in love. Candidly, I did not care if he pastored a little church or a large church. I was simply committed to him as a friend.

While on vacation with Cristie, I received an emergency call from my friend. He told me he was resigning the following Sunday and then asked if I would begin a new ministry with him. "Hold on," I said. "What is going on?" His son later told me that, for years, he had had an extramarital affair with the wife of a close friend. Finally, it had all caught up with him. I was so sad to hear what had happened, and cordially declined a joint opportunity to work together.

My pastor friend ended up pursuing a

business career in a city near where my wife was raised. Consequently, it afforded me the opportunity to keep in touch with him as we visited Cristie's parents. Several times, we went to lunch. He would often say, "I am making so much money now. It is great! I had no idea how much pressure I was under as a pastor." As he would boast, I wanted to say to him, "I don't care if you make a lot of money or a little, you are my friend, and I am always going to be your friend."

Looking back, I realize I was not there when he needed me. A business associate left him in a precarious situation. One day, in desperation, he drove to a cemetery and took a gun to his head. After struggling for several minutes, he finally died. His suicide sent shock waves across the nation. I felt so bad. Cristie and I have wept several times together, asking ourselves, "Why didn't we see it coming? Why didn't we ask him if he was depressed?" Simply, "Why didn't we take more of an interest in his life?" I have wondered why he didn't call me, and tell me about the problems in which he had found himself. We both knew enough people that we could have put our heads together and remedied any burden. In retrospect, the tragedy of his life motivates me to tell *you* to be on the lookout when your friend is hurting. Take time to listen. You don't want to carry a memory, like I have, the rest of your life. Let me tell you how to rescue your friend or family member, should they be struggling, as was my friend.

> *1. Read the signals.* Take an interest. When a friend or family member is exhibiting behavior that is dangerous and reflective of depression, make yourself more available and more interested than ever. People cocooned in problems really feel like no one cares. Through this book, we keep hearing the words *hopelessness* and *helplessness*. In a sense, the suicidal person feels helpless to change his or her deep depression. A loving friend or family member can make all the difference. It requires you to read the signals. It will require you to slow your life down long enough to care, and care enough to confront.

A young girl named Dee, said, "I am alive today because my best friend would not leave me alone. I was going downhill, and I kept telling her to leave me alone, and she kept saying things like, 'Real friends don't leave when their friends are in trouble.' I really did not want her to leave, but I didn't think anyone cared for me."

What if you don't know, for sure, whether or

not there is a life-threatening problem lurking inside your friend? Don't take chances! One expert counseled: "Even if you're not completely sure about the seriousness of the depression in yourself or a friend, it is better to take the necessary steps and find out you were wrong, than to say nothing and find out you were right."[21]

> *2. Be a detective.* I am not suggesting you stalk your friend, or steal a glance at their personal diary; but I am saying to be on the lookout for problems, or potential problems. The best way to accomplish this is by encouraging your friend to talk, whenever you sense something wrong.

What can you ask? If your friend has not seemed well lately, ask something like, "You don't seem like yourself. Is there anything you would like to talk about?" If they say yes, and tell you about negative feelings and thoughts, do not hesitate to ask if these include thoughts of suicide. "When in doubt, check it out. If you are suspicious, ask the person directly," says family counselor Cynthia Taylor.[22]

If your friend admits to thinking about suicide, your next step is to ask, "Do you have a plan?" If the answer is affirmative, get the details. The more specific the details, the more serious the situation. More about this in a minute.

Being a good detective demands knowledge of the suicide warning signs. Review Chapter 3, "Warning Signs," periodically.

> **3. Listen carefully.** Your suicidal friend must know someone is willing to truly listen. Chances are your friend will feel no one at home is tuned in, so you have to show *you are.* An insightful report in the *FBI Law Enforcement Bulletin* said:

> "Many suicidal young people have the inability, or lack of opportunity, to express their unhappiness, frustration or failure. They find their efforts to express their feelings are either totally unacceptable to their parents, ignored or met by defensive hostility. This response then drives the child into further isolation, reinforcing the belief of something being terribly wrong."[17]

In Omaha, Nebraska, where five students in the same high school attempted suicide in less than two weeks (three died by suicide), other teenagers became concerned and got involved. A network of listeners was organized to avert more tragedy. Plano, Texas, experienced 11 teenage suicides in just 16 months, and students set up BIONIC (Believe It or Not I Care) and SWAT (Students

Working All Together) networks. Through these organizations, they befriended newly-transferred or depressed classmates. Adults created a 24-hour hotline. The payoff? Teen suicides slowed and clusters virtually ceased.

As you listen, remember that your friend may be pointed—or very vague. Verbally, they might make direct references to killing themselves by asking, "What would you do if I were to kill myself?" Indirectly, they might say, "Everyone will be better off without me," or "You won't have to worry about me much longer." Any reference to dying must be taken seriously.

> *4. Say the right things.* Remember that asking a person about suicide will not plant the idea in his or her mind. In fact, your question says, "I've been paying attention to you and I see something's wrong." One author explains:

"It is not unusual for teenagers to respond, 'No. Are you crazy?' It is their way of protecting themselves from the possibility of being rejected, ridiculed, or treated as if they are crazy. Never settle for the first 'no.' Pursue it with words of understanding such as, 'Look, with everything happening in your life (list the incidents) and with the way you have been feeling, it is normal to feel like ending it all. It's not crazy. So, have you thought about it?' This shows you are serious, care, understand, and are free to talk about it. If they have been thinking about it, they are likely to tell after this. If they are are not suicidal, they will still respect the caring and concern and be more liable to come for help when in trouble."[18]

Here are some right things to say to a friend you think might be thinking suicidal thoughts:

- "I didn't know how serious things have become. Let's talk about it."

- "It sounds like you are feeling totally hopeless. I understand how you can feel like this. Have you told anyone else? We have to talk to someone about this."

- "I don't want you to do anything to hurt yourself. I don't know how we can change the feeling, but I know there are people who can help."

- "I can't watch you 24 hours a day. If you want to, you will find a way, but I do not want you to, and I will do anything to keep you from killing yourself."

- "I want to hear everything that has been happening. I have time." (Be sure you do, and be willing to drop everything if you don't.)

- "Abusing drugs and alcohol, like you are doing, shows there must be some inner pain you are trying to medicate. Is everything okay? Will you let me help you and get help?"

Now, it is equally important, too, to know what *not* to say. Here are a few statements to avoid:

- "You will get over it. Things will be better tomorrow." (Things may be better tomorrow, and making this kind of promise may make you part of the problem, rather than part of the solution.)

- "You have your whole life ahead of you." (The suicidal person is usually convinced that the 'whole life ahead' is bleak and not worth living. This could prove to be a statement of demotivation, to make a person actually think about suicide. In essence, it says, "Do you know how miserable you are feeling right now? Well, let me encourage you by reminding you that you are going to feel this way the rest of your life!" Weigh your words.)

- "You don't really feel that way." (Yes,

the suicidal person *does* feel that way. Don't allow your pride or ignorance to be showcased in the presence of someone else's emotional pain.)

- "You would never do it." (How do you know? That is almost like saying, "I dare you to try." Over 50,000 teenagers in the United States and over 2,000 teenagers in Canada completed suicide in just the past ten years!)

So, the bottom line is: Don't criticize, judge, ridicule, minimize, expose your ignorance and insensitivity, or promise anything you can't deliver.

5. Take action. A suicidal threat is not like your morning alarm clock. You can't push a snooze button and wait a while longer before you do something. I know a number of parents who knew they needed to intervene in their children's lives—but they waited. These parents knew, deep down, their son or daughter was in trouble, but they did not muster the fortitude to do what needed to be done in time. Please don't join their company. When there is clear suicidal inclination exhibited and expressed, it's a call for immediate action.

- Tell your friend about the resources for help. Take a look in the back of this book— one of the most effective suicide hotlines is **1-800-273-TALK (8255)**. There also may be a local suicide hotline in your area. Remember, the Crossroads ministry toll-free Prayer Lines are available 24/7, where caring people are ready to pray with you, or the person for whom you are concerned, at 1-866-273-4444. This essential call centre has been used to rescue precious people in their neediest moments in life. Friends are standing by right now to take your call. Don't be hesitant. If you have a friend in need, help make the call with them.

- It is best that your friend make the decision themselves to seek professional help, but be willing to help make the arrangements and go along to lend your support. I have been asked to lead interventions on people when the whole family felt inadequate. These are very difficult situations. In one situation, a young lady, who had been a model, had descended into the depths of drug and alcohol abuse. Her desperate family asked for my help—but cautioned me she could be volatile. Candy was shocked, when I entered their home, and told her we loved her so much, we were not going to stand back and let her die. Hours later, we checked her into a reputable facility to help her get back on the road to recovery. She is alive today. Generally, these surprise intervention sessions need someone with experience to lead them— but not always. When there is solidarity in a family, regarding the conviction that a brother or sister, mom or dad is dying, and the family refuses to stand by and let it happen, that's generally all it takes. I am aware this is a highly stressful situation, but an intervention is far less stressful than living the rest of your life knowing your child took his or her own life.

- If a specific suicide plan has been revealed, be prepared to remove the instruments of the method if possible. *Note to parents:* I want to caution you about easy access to guns in the home. If your son or daughter is suicidal, those weapons should be under lock and key. We have too many weapons, and too much easy access for firearms. Remember, the number one method of suicide is the use of firearms.

- Establish a binding agreement with your friend. Cynthia Taylor suggested: "Ask for a verbal contract that he or she will contact you, or another designated person, if he or she has thoughts about suicide, or an inclination to complete suicide."[19]

- Pray before, during, and after your encounter with a suicidal friend.

- If your friend refuses to get help, contact someone with expertise. Ask for his or her advice and direction in the situation. Crisis intervention counselors will tell you that, deep down, a suicidal person wants someone who can reach out with help, even when they appear to reject it. If you have made a promise of secrecy with regard to someone's expressed desire to complete suicide, break it for the sake of the person's life. Keeping a friend is more important than keeping your word, when he or she is teetering on the brink of life or death.

If you fail to act when a friend is in grave danger and your friend completes suicide, you will be haunted for years by the ghost of guilt. Don't let that happen. Sometimes, I am overwhelmed by what teenagers tell me they are going through. They open up to me, I suppose, because in many cases I am the first person they have heard address the problems plaguing their hearts. I tell teenagers everywhere, listen to your friends. Some of them are in real danger and you don't know it. Let me share a letter I received from Bridgette in Colorado:

I have been really having a lot of problems ... Over the summer, a lot of my friends, who I looked up to, turned to drugs and drinking. Right now, I am caught in the middle of a lot of things. One girl tried to commit suicide and is now paralyzed. I have been thinking about getting on drugs again. That really scares me, but I have really been thinking about it ... Well, right now I am really thinking about suicide. I have cut my wrists a couple of times. But so far, I haven't found a foolproof plan. Right now I don't think I have the courage. But with each passing day, I get a little more. I see a real problem coming. I am reaching out to you. Please help.

Remember I told you how the dynamic, international ministry of Crossroads (**crossroads.ca**), based in Burlington, Ontario, Canada, has caring, toll-free Prayer Lines, dedicated to take your calls, day and night, at

1-866-273-4444. I want you to know that caring people are standing by, right now, to help you discover life and fulfillment. Our ministry prayer partners have been successful in their mission. There is hope for you. You are only one phone call away. Call us today; write the number down, either for yourself or a friend: 1-866-273-4444.

CHAPTER 7

STARTING ALL OVER

Standing right next to me, Cindy asked, "Jerry, do you know Jesus?" I couldn't believe her interest in me. Did she know I was almost dead 11 weeks earlier?

Do you remember my story back in Chapter 2? My parents had bribed me to go to a Christian youth camp by promising me a professional foosball table for my birthday. Even though they weren't Christians, they knew something had to change, because they were losing me. I had been at the end of my rope— barely hanging on to life.

At the time, my family was a wreck. My mom was an alcoholic. My poor dad was on the verge of a heart attack, trying to mediate five sons, all the time knowing I was on the verge of suicide. My older brother, Jeff, had run away from home and met a junkie and hitched trains to California. That junkie had turned him on to some heavy drugs. Jeff was being pushed down a four-lane highway in a shopping cart, high, in the state of California, when the police picked him up. My mom had flown out to get him and bring him back home. Life was tough and uncertain for the Johnston family. I told you about the last night of Windermere Christian camp, Thursday, June 21— the night when Cindy, a beautiful girl I had admired all week, invited me to go up to the second row and sit with her—and my entire life changed. Without me knowing, a group of young people had been praying for me all week and had gone to the camp speaker and asked him to do the same.

It was a little peculiar, sitting on that second row with Cindy. I had never sat near the front before. The speaker, Bob, seemed so close, and for once, I decided to listen. He shared how God loved each and every person. He told us how God demonstrated His love by sending Jesus Christ to live, die, and rise again from the dead—so He could forgive the sin of *anyone* who would come to Him, by faith, and invite Him into his or her heart and life.

I had never heard that message before. Our posh Johnson County church was such a turn off that I had never listened. My brothers and I used to have candle fights at the Christmas Eve services and see if we could light one another on fire.

That night at camp, I realized I had never invited Jesus Christ into my life. No wonder I was so empty ... so filled with despair, always searching for something to fill the emptiness in my heart. The camp speaker quoted John 3:16, "For God so loved the world that He gave His only begotten Son, that whoever believes in Him, should not perish, but have everlasting life." Bob made it clear—you don't go to heaven by just attending church or being a good person: you have to receive Jesus Christ into your heart. You have to invite Him into your life.

At the end of his talk, the camp speaker invited everyone in the audience who wanted to receive Christ to come forward. Music was playing and my heart was pounding. For the first time in my life, it was as if God was speaking directly to me.

Standing right next to me, Cindy asked, "Jerry, do you know Jesus?" I couldn't believe her interest in me. Did she know I was almost dead eleven weeks earlier?

With God helping me, I left my seat and walked to the front. That night, I prayed a prayer that changed my life and began my new life with

Christ. Would you pray this prayer with me, too?

Dear God,

Thank you for sending Jesus Christ to die on the cross, paying the price for my sin. I believe Jesus rose from the dead. Right now, by faith, I invite Jesus to come into my heart and please forgive me of my sins. Thank you that I am forgiven, and am now Your child.

In Jesus' Name,

Amen

In an instant, internally, I knew something happened at the very moment I prayed that prayer! Christ had come into my heart. I had become a Christian, and it felt so good! Later that night, I found the camp speaker, Bob, in his room and told him my whole story. He encouraged me to go home and live for God. He told me to tell my parents and friends that I was a new person … a child of God.

I could not wait to get home. I already told you about my friend with the Camaro. I jumped in and we drove nearly 100-miles-an-hour on the way home, so I could tell my mom and dad that I was a "new Jerry." When I entered the front door of our suburban home, I hollered as loud as I could, "Mom and Dad, I am home. Come down here I have to tell you something." My Dad was startled, wondering what I was up to now. Quickly they assembled themselves in our family room.

"Dad, Mom, I am a Christian! Jesus Christ lives in my heart! Everything is brand new. The emptiness is gone! I don't want to do drugs anymore."

Mom started crying. Dad did too. I could tell something brand new was beginning in our home that very moment. Darkness was leaving and the light of Christ was illuminating every inch of our home.

That first Sunday, the pastor of Teresa's (my brother's fiancé's) church, shelved his sermon and invited the youth who had gone to camp to share a testimony in the Sunday morning service. I had never heard of that word "testimony." In anticipation, the night before, I had had my Mom iron a shirt and get me some nice pants to wear, instead of those jeans I used to live in and get high in. Sunday morning, I had my dad tie a red bow-tie on me!

After a few teenagers shared, I left my seat and climbed the stairs of the church platform and told the entire congregation how Jesus Christ had changed my life and how I was going to share Jesus with everyone I knew! Mom and dad were crying. Both of them went forward that morning and gave their hearts to Jesus Christ.

I started a Youth for Christ club for my school, and in one year, we led over 200 of our classmates to faith in Christ. It was my job, every Monday night at the YFC Club, to give the invitation for teens to receive Christ. I fell so in love with seeing people coming to Christ, that I have been sharing the Gospel ever since.

If you have never received Christ, let me urge you to pray the same prayer I did. And when you do, write me or call our Prayer Line at 1-866-273-4444 and tell one of our counselors you prayed to receive Jesus Christ. Walk with God. Read the Bible. Grow in your relationship with Christ. The Christian walk is not a bed of roses, but you will never walk alone, or face any of your problems—alone—again.

CROSSROADS CENTRE PRAYER LINES

Depressed? Feel all alone? Do you need to talk to someone? We are waiting, 24/7. The call is free.

1-866-273-4444

crossroads.ca

Since the very first broadcast of *100 Huntley Street* on June 15, 1977, the Prayer Lines have played a key role in what takes place through Crossroads as instant two-way communication, making immediate response possible. From that first program where people called to receive Jesus Christ as their Savior and Lord, follow-up was an important and integral part of this ministry. Follow-up then became *follow through,* in connecting these precious people to caring churches throughout the nation. Now over 35 years later, with millions of calls received and thousands of salvation decisions for Jesus Christ recorded, the immediacy of response continues through the Prayer Lines. Now, online access to our Crossroads website opens a whole new realm of contact worldwide!

At the Crossroads Prayer Centre, desperate, broken and suicidal people find the hope and help they so crave. Here they are introduced to the reality that "the Lord is close to the brokenhearted and saves those who are crushed in spirit." *(Psalm 34:18)* Rather than being told God is far from them because they are broken, just the opposite is true. His Word declares He is "close to the brokenhearted," and that is liberation, an invitation to draw near this caring Lord! Here in the Crossroads Prayer Centre we have come to understand that Jesus is the "wounded healer" *(Isaiah 53:5)* who comes to us in our own woundedness. Amazingly, as we allow His woundedness to touch ours, healing takes place. Over time, and as we give him permission to work in our lives, we then become "wounded healers" to others through the very grace and healing we have received from Jesus! The invitation of Jesus in Matthew 11:28-30 is one we continually declare through the Prayer Centre to our broken world: *"Come to me, all you who are weary and burdened, and I will give you rest. Take my yoke upon you and learn from me, for I am gentle and humble in heart, and you will find rest for your souls. For my yoke is easy and my burden is light."* The Message says it like this: "Are you tired? Worn out? Burned out on religion? Come to me. Get away with me and you'll recover your life. I'll show you how to take a real rest. Walk with me and work with me—watch how I do it. Learn the unforced rhythms of grace. I won't lay anything heavy or ill-fitting on you. Keep company with me and you'll learn to live freely and lightly."

Have you come to Him? If not, allow your brokenness to be the key in allowing you to discover. He is near. We are waiting to love and help you.

END NOTES

a Dobson, Dr. James. *Children At Risk*. Thomas Nelson, 1994.

1 "Mental Health—Depression," Health Canada: www.hc-sc.gc.ca/hl-vs/iyh-vsv/diseases-maladies/depression-eng.php#ba (accessed August 22, 2012).

2 *"Improving Early Identification & Treatment of Adolescent Depression: Considerations & Strategies for Health Plans,"* NIHCM Foundation Issue Brief, February 2010. http://nihcm.org/pdf/Adol_MH_Issue_Brief_Final.pdf (access August 22, 2012).

3 Tim LaHaye, *How to Win Over Depression* (Grand Rapids, MI: Zondervan, 1979), 24.

4 Dan Elliott and Nicholas Riccardi, "James Holmes, Aurora Shooting Suspect, Made Threats Months Before 'Dark Knight' Massacre, Prosecutors Say." *Huffington Post*, August 24, 2012: www.huffingtonpost.com/2012/08/24/James-holmes-threats-aurora-colorado_n_1828616.html (accessed August 25, 2012).

5 Peter Langman, "Dylan Kelbold's Journal and Other Writings," www.schoolshooters.info/

dylan-klebold-journal.pdf (accessed August 22, 2012).

[6] Susan Klebold, "I Will Never Know Why," *Oprah Magazine*, November, 2009. www.oprah.com/world/Susan-Klebolds-O-Magazine-Essay-I-Will-Never-Know-Why/1 (accessed August 22, 2012).

[7] "Basement Tapes" March 15, 1999, Evidence item #265, http://acolumbinesite.com/quotes1.html (accessed August 22, 2012).

[8] "Youth Suicidal Behavior—Fact Sheet," *American Association of Suicidology:* www.suicidology.org/c/document_library/get_file?folderld=248&name=DLFE-416.pdf (accessed August 23, 2012).

[9] Web-based Injury Statistics Query and Reporting System (WISQARS), 2010. *Centers for Disease Control and Prevention (CDC):* www.cdc.gov/injury/wisqars/index.html (accessed August 21, 2012).

[10] David Shaffer, *Teenage Suicide.* National Alliance of Mental Illness, www.nami.org/Content/ContentGroups/Helpline1/Teenage_Suicide.htm (accessed August 23, 2012).

[11] SK Goldsmith, TC Pellmar, AM Kleinman, WE Bunney, editors. *Reducing Suicide: a*

national imperative. Washington, DC: National Academy Press, 2002.

[12] About Suicide, Canadian Association for Suicide Prevention. www.suicideprevention.ca/about-suicide/ (accessed August 20, 2012).

[13] "Suicide rates: An overview," in Health at a Glance, www.statcan.gc.ca/pub/82-624-x/2012001/article/11696-eng.htm (accessed August 20, 2012).

[14] Marcia Seligson, "Are You Suicidal?" *Harper's Bazaar* (August 1972), 63.

[15] N. L. Farberow, Some Facts About Suicide (Washington, D.C.: U. S. Government Printing Office, 1961), 12.

[16] "Suicide in the U.S.: Statistics and Prevention," *The National Institute of Mental Health*, www.nimh.nih.gov/health/publications/suicide-in-the-us-statistics-and-prevention/index (access August 20, 2012).

[17] Robert J. Barry, "Teenage Suicide: An American Tragedy," *FBI Law Enforcement Bulletin* (April 1986), 17.

[18] William Steele, "Preventing the Spread of Suicide Among Adolescents," *USA Today Magazine* (November 1985), 59.

[19] Taylor, 32.

BIBLIOGRAPHY

BOOKS

Goldsmith, SK, TC Pellmar, AM Kleinman, WE Bunney, eds. *Reducing Suicide: a national imperative.* Washington, DC: National Academy Press, 2002.

Farberow, N. L. *Some Facts About Suicide.* Washington, D.C.: U. S. Government Printing Office, 1961.

Mann, Peggy. *Marijuana Alert.* New York: McGraw-Hill, 1985.

LaHaye, Tim. *How to Win Over Depression.* Grand Rapids, MI: Zondervan, 1979.

ARTICLES

Barry, Robert J. "Teenage Suicide: An American Tragedy." *FBI Law Enforcement Bulletin,* April 1986.

Breu, Giovanna. "When Hopelessness Sets In, Warns Psychiatrist Aaron Beck, Suicide Can Be Close Behind." *People,* April 7, 1986.

Cantor, Pamela. "Schools Must Help These Tragedies." *USA Today,* Feb 26, 1986. Accessed

Sept 5, 2012.

Colt, George Howard. "The Enigma of Suicide." *Harvard Magazine*, Sept-Oct 1983.

Elliott, Dan and Nicholas Riccardi. "James Holmes, Aurora Shooting Suspect, Made Threats Months Before 'Dark Knight' Massacre, Prosecutors Say." *Huffington Post*, Aug 24, 2012: www.huffingtonpost.com/2012/08/24/James-holmes-threats-aurora-colorado_n_1828616.html (accessed August 25, 2012).

Helms, Sally and Robert Tenenbaum. "Kids and Sex." *Columbus Monthly*, November 1981.

Klebold, Susan. "I Will Never Know Why." *Oprah Magazine*, Nov, 2009. www.oprah.com/world/Susan-Klebolds-O-Magazine-Essay-I-Will-Never-Know-Why/1 (accessed August 22, 2012).

Langlois, Christine. "Teen Sexuality." *Canadian Living*. www.canadianliving.com/moms/family_life/teen_sexuality.php (accessed Sept 4, 2012).

Meehan, Bob with Stephen J. Meyer. "Is Your Child Taking Drugs?" *Reader's Digest*, July 1986.

Seligson, Marcia. "Are You Suicidal?" *Harper's Bazaar*, August 1972.

Stack, Steven. "A Leveling Off in Young Suicide."

The Wall Street Journal, May 28, 1986.

Steele, William. "Preventing the Spread of Suicide Among Adolescents." *USA Today Magazine*, November 1985.

Taylor, Cynthia. "Helping the Suicidal." *Eternity*, March 1985.

"Alcohol causes 2.5 million death a year: WHO." *CBC News*, Feb 11, 2011, www.cbc.ca/news/health/story/2011/02/11/health-alcohol-deaths.html. Accessed Sept 4, 2012.

"CDC report shows about 112 million annual incidents of people drinking and driving Centers." *U.S. Center for Disease Control and Prevention*, October 2011. www.cdc.gov/media/releases/2011/p1004_drinking_driving.html. Accessed Sept 4, 2012.

"Survey Shows Drug-Infested US High Schools." *The Fix*. www.thefix.com/content/drugs-us-high-schools90497. Accessed September 5, 2012.

"The Games Teenagers Play." *Newsweek*, September 1, 1980.

WEBSITES AND STUDIES

About Suicide, Canadian Association for Suicide

Prevention. www.suicideprevention.ca/about-suicide/ (accessed August 20, 2012).

"Alcohol Addiction," www.alcoholaddiction.info/alcoholism-statistics.htm (accessed Sept 4, 2012).

"Basement Tapes" March 15, 1999, Evidence item #265, http://acolumbinesite.com/quotes1.html (accessed August 22, 2012).

Centers for Disease Control and Prevention (CDC): www.cdc.gov/injury/wisqars/index.html (accessed August 21, 2012).

"Improving Early Identification & Treatment of Adolescent Depression: Considerations & Strategies for Health Plans," *NIHCM Foundation Issue Brief,* February 2010. http://nihcm.org/pdf/Adol_MH_Issue_Brief_Final.pdf (accessed August 22, 2012).

Langman, Peter. "Dylan Kelbold's Journal and Other Writings." www.schoolshooters.info/dylan-klebold-journal.pdf (accessed August 22, 2012).

"Mental Health – Depression," *Health Canada*: www.hc-sc.gc.ca/hl-vs/iyh-vsv/diseases-maladies/depression-eng.php#ba (accessed August 22, 2012).

"Nightline," *ABC Network* (November 1984).

"Sexual Intercourse," *Youth Risk Behavior Surveillance.* The U.S. Center for Disease Control and Prevention, www.sexedlibrary.org/index.cfm?pageId=815 (accessed September 4, 2012).

Shaffer, David. *Teenage Suicide.* National Alliance of Mental Illness, www.nami.org/Content/ContentGroups/Helpline1/Teenage_Suicide.htm (accessed August 23, 2012).

"Substance Use by Canadian Youth - A National Survey of Canadians' Use of Alcohol and Other Drugs - Canadian Addiction Survey," *Health Canada*, http://goo.gl/PTQve (accessed Sept 5, 2012).

"Suicide in the U.S.: Statistics and Prevention," *The National Institute of Mental Health,* www.nimh.nih.gov/health/publications/suicide-in-the-us-statistics-and-prevention/index (access August 20, 2012).

"Suicide rates: An overview," in *Health at a Glance*, www.statcan.gc.ca/pub/82-624-x/2012001/article/11696-eng.htm (accessed August 20, 2012).

"Teen Drivers: Fact Sheet." *Centers for Disease Control and Prevention*, www.cdc.gov/motorvehiclesafety/teen_drivers/teendrivers_

factsheet.html (accessed Sept 4, 2012).

Paglia-Boak, Angela, Robert E. Mann, Edward M. Adlaf, and Jürgen Rehm. *Drug Use Among Ontario Students 2009 Study* (CAMH), http://goo.gl/Travy.

"Youth Suicidal Behavior – Fact Sheet," *American Association of Suicidology:* www.suicidology.org/c/document_library/get_file?folderld=248&name=DLFE-416.pdf (accessed August 23, 2012).

PROFILE: JERRY JOHNSTON, D. MIN.

Jerry Johnston (Doctor of Ministry—Acadia University Divinity College, Wolfville, Nova Scotia) has captivated over 4,000,000 youth on more than 2,500 public school campuses, addressing vital issues. He has held events in over 1,200 churches of all denominations throughout the United States and Canada. Over 125,000 people have come to faith in Jesus Christ through his invitation. Jerry has authored 12 books and produced 12 videos that have been distributed to thousands of churches. He has presented 112 different popular teaching series comprised of over 900 expositional messages on video, many of which are available online.

While still in high school, Jerry's ministry career began as an Evangelist-at-Large for Youth for Christ, the same ministry that launched Billy Graham. Later, Jerry was awarded an Honorary Doctor of Divinity degree (1997).

Dr. Johnston has extensive media experience and has been interviewed on *Fox News' The O'Reilly Factor*, *Good Morning America*, *World News Tonight*, *Nightline*; *The Today Show*, CNN's *Crossfire*, Deborah Norville Tonight, MSNBC's

Scarborough Country, *Connected Coast to Coast with Ron Reagan, Focus on the Family, The 700 Club, 100 Huntley Street* in Canada, and many others.

Jerry's wife, Dr. Cristie Jo Johnston, is an effective teacher of God's Word who has broad appeal to both men and women. The Johnston's have three children: Danielle, married to Christian Newsome, senior pastor of The Journey Church, Lee's Summit, MO; Jeremiah Johnston, Ph.D. (cand.), Lecturer in Biblical Studies, Acadia Divinity College, married to Audrey; and Jenilee, married to Jeffrey Mullikin.

Jerry has served as an effective consultant to pastors and various ministries on media development, fundraising, and mentoring leaders.

To schedule Jerry to speak in your church, school, or area write or call:

In Canada:
Crossroads
Box 5100
Burlington, ON
L74 4M2

In the United States:
Crossroads
P. O. Box 486
Niagara Falls, NY
14302

905-332-6400, ext. 3231

jerryjohnston.com

Jerry Johnston on Twitter:
twitter.com/Jerry_Johnston

Jerry Johnston on Facebook:
facebook.com/DrJerryJohnston

PROFILE:
DON SIMMONDS

As Chairman and CEO of Crossroads, Don brings a blend of experiences in both business and ministry. In a media dominated society, he believes strongly that God's love for people needs to be presented in a relevant way through the power of today's media technology.

Don and his wife Fay have been married for 37 years and live in Uxbridge, Ontario. They have four children. Shauna (29), Craig (26), Brett (25) and April (15). With their love for God and commitment to family as overriding priorities, Don and Fay have enjoyed a full life focused on two of the most rapidly changing environments: the electronics business and the teenage world.

In business Don is known as a *"serial entrepreneur"*, having been involved in over 20 new ventures in the last 30 years. The businesses cover a diverse range of ideas from consumer audio products to solar electric power to dairy farming! Don was one of seven partners that started the Lenbrook Group in 1977, a private business incubation company perhaps best known for having created Clearnet, one of Canada's wireless networks sold in 2001 to Telus.

Until 2007 Don was the founding CEO of AirIQ Inc., a business providing wireless GPS tracking for all types of vehicles and marine vessels. During his years as CEO, AirIQ was named one of Canada's fastest growing technology companies in the Deloitte Canadian Technology Fast 500 Program and ranked 12th and 17th in PROFIT magazine's ranking of Canada's Fastest-Growing Companies for 2005, 2006. Don was a finalist in the Ernst & Young Entrepreneur Of The Year® Awards in 2005.

Don and his wife Fay have been youth leaders at their church in Uxbridge for many years. From 1991-1994 Don left the business environment to work more intensely with youth as the National Youth Coordinator for Canadian Baptists and then enjoyed being the Executive Director of Toronto Youth for Christ (now Youth Unlimited). From 1980 to 1990 Don served as Canada's representative to Baptist World Alliance Youth and assisted in the planning of world youth conferences in Argentina, Scotland and Zimbabwe.

Don enjoys being a private pilot, serves on a number of profit and not for profit boards, and particularly appreciates the opportunity to coach the young men on the Uxbridge Tigers

High School Hockey team whose motto is
"winning at hockey and winning in life!"

To schedule Don to speak in your church,
school, or area write or call:

Crossroads
Box 5100
Burlington, Ontario
 L74 4M2

905-332-6400, ext. 3307

FOR FURTHER HELP

Suicide Hotline

1-800-273-TALK (8255)

Canadian Mental Health Association:
cmha.ca

Health Canada: **hc-sc.gr.ca**

Suicide Education and Information Centre:
suicideinfo.ca

Statistics Canada: **statcan.gc.ca**

World Health Organization: **who.int**

International Association of Suicide Prevention:
iasp.into

American Academy of Child & Adolescent

Psychiatry

3615 Wisconsin Ave., NW

Washington, DC 20016-3007

202-966-7300

aacap.org

American Association of Suicidology

4201 Connecticut Ave., NW

Washington, DC 20008

202-237-2280

suicidology.org

American Foundation for Suicide Prevention

120 Wall Street, 22nd Floor

New York, NY 10005

888-333-AFSP (2377)

afsp.org

SAVE (Suicide Awareness Voices of Education)

8120 Penn Ave. S., Suite 470

Bloomington, MN 55431

952-946-7998

save.org

SPAN-USA (Suicide Prevention Advocacy Network)

1025 Vermont Ave., NW, Suite 1066

Washington, DC 20005

202-449-3600

spanusa.org

Yellow Ribbon Suicide Prevention Program

P. O. Box 644

Westminster, CO 80030-0644

303-429-3530

yellowribbon.org